CAREERS IN MARKETING

1993–1994 EDITION

Joel R. Evans
Hofstra University

Barry Berman
Hofstra University

MACMILLAN PUBLISHING COMPANY
New York

MAXWELL MACMILLAN CANADA, INC.
Toronto

MAXWELL MACMILLAN INTERNATIONAL
New York   Oxford   Singapore   Sydney

Macmillan Publishing Company
866 Third Avenue, New York, New York 10022

Macmillan Publishing Company is part of the
Maxwell Communications Group of Companies.

Maxwell Macmillan Canada, Inc.
1200 Eglinton Avenue East
Suite 200
Don Mills, Ontario M3C 3N1

ISBN   0-02-334280-3

Printing: 3 4 5 6 7 8   Year: 3 4 5 6 7 8 9 0 1

CONTENTS

CHAPTER ONE

PLANNING FOR YOUR FUTURE

INTRODUCTION

Getting ready for and finding your first career-oriented job should be a key goal as you advance through college and get ready for graduation. Thus, it is important that you begin thinking about the career you would like to pursue by your junior year and begin preparing for the job search process to embark on such a career as early as possible in your senior year. You must be serious in your approach and devote enough time to these activities. As an underclassman, it is wise to think ahead and develop your credentials.

Career planning is also critical when there is a slow-growth economy, you desire a position in an industry with a large amount of applicants relative to the number of avail-able positions (such as advertising), and you need to travel to take interviews. Too often, students do not plan far enough ahead to prepare the credentials and the job search strategy that are needed to compete in the marketplace. Many of these students may find themselves unemployed for six months to a year after graduation, may accept part-time rather than full-time work, or may end up working on jobs that are not related to their ultimate career objectives.

The career preparation process may be broken down into these general steps: knowing yourself, developing contacts, writing the resumé and associated cover letter, interviewing, and follow-ups. These are discussed in the following sections.

KNOWING YOURSELF

The first thing that you should do in planning for your future is a personal assessment, which involves critically examining your strengths and weaknesses, likes and dislikes, and long-term goals. These are examples of the types of questions you should ask yourself:

1. What are my greatest strengths?
2. What are my greatest weaknesses?
3. What types of activities do I most like doing?
4. What types of activities do I least like doing?
5. Do I like working with people? With numbers? With computers?
6. Am I a self-starter or do I need close supervision?
7. Do I want a career that will constantly challenge me?
8. Do I have the potential to supervise people?
9. What are my long-term career goals in terms of job advancement? In terms of earnings?
10. How important is career success to me? Will my career be

more important to me than anything else?
11. Would I rather work in a large or a small company?
12. Would I like to eventually work for myself?
13. Am I willing to relocate to get a good job?
14. In ten years, would I be unhappy if I did not hold a top management position?
15. What would be my ideal entry-level, career-oriented job?
16. For what entry-level, career-oriented job am I the best qualified?
17. What should I do to bridge the gap between questions 15 and 16?
18. How flexible am I in my career options?

DEVELOPING CONTACTS

You need to be aggressive in developing contacts during your job search. In addition to writing to or telephoning the potential employers and professional/trade associations cited in Chapters Four and Five of this book, you should study sources of job listings like those indicated in Table 1.

You should also speak with your college placement office, former employers, professors, parents of friends, and relatives for leads. Although you may feel awkward in asking for contacts, in many cases, these people may be aware of job openings that are not advertised and they may be able to steer you to the right person in a particular firm. Friends, family members, and acquaintances are generally happy to help.

One common mistake that some students make is to schedule too heavy a course load during their senior year of college. As a result, they have too little time to devote to the job search. A lighter load in your senior year (which might mean going to summer school at the end of the junior year) will allow you to generate sufficient contacts.

WRITING YOUR RESUMÉ AND COVER LETTER

Your resumé is one of the most important documents in the job search. It summarizes your education, experience, and other accomplishments, and should strive to differentiate you from your classmates.

A good resumé needs to "stand out from the crowd" by highlighting how your distinctive background will best fit the needs of the potential employer. It should accurately portray your accomplishments without being boastful. You must realize that the resumé is a marketing tool and that it will often be your first communication with a potential employer. As the old adage goes, you often cannot fix a bad first impression.

There are five steps in the resumé process: (1) preparing a resumé data sheet, (2) developing a rough draft of your resumé, (3) arranging for the final copy of your resumé to be

Table 1

Selected Sources of Job Leads For Marketing Positions

The classified sections of *Advertising Age, New York Times, Wall Street Journal,* and local newspapers. If you plan to relocate, try to buy the local newspaper of your planned destination. Arrange for the newspaper to mail copies at your current address. The *Marketing News* and newsletters of local American Marketing Association chapters also have job listings.

CPC Annual. This is generally available at your college placement office.

Peterson's Job Opportunities for Business and Liberal Arts Graduates. This is generally available at your college library or bookstore.

Occupational Outlook Handbook. This is a standard reference book that describes average salaries, career paths, and the outlook for a large number of job titles in marketing. This is generally available at your college library.

General directories of companies. There are a large number of directories of firms. Annual issues of *Fortune, Forbes,* and *Business Week* list key data on company sales and profits. These directories also list data such as the firms' main office locations and phone numbers. Look for special issues: "Fortune 500 Industrials," "Fortune Service 500," "Forbes 500," and "Business Week 1000." In addition, listings of larger companies and descriptive material are available in Standard & Poor's, Moody's and Value Line directories. Smaller firms can be found in *Dun & Bradstreet's Middle Market Directory* and in *Inc.*'s "Inc. 500." These directories are generally available at your college library.

Specific company directories. For general marketing careers, refer to the *1992 Marketing News International Directory of the American Marketing Association and Marketing Services Guide.* For retailing, see *Fairchild's Financial Manual of Retail Stores.* In marketing research, see the annual *Green Book: The International Directory of Marketing Research Companies and Services.* For advertising, see the monthly *Standard Directory of Advertising Agencies.* For shopping centers, see the annual *Shopping Center Directory.* For international marketing careers, see the *U.S. Importers and Exporters Directory.* These directories are usually available at your college library.

---

printed, (4) preparing the cover letter, and (5) the resumé follow-up. Specific hints relative to the resumé process at each stage are discussed next. A sample marketing resumé is also shown.

Preparing A Resumé Data Sheet

A resumé data sheet should be used as a guide you when developing your resumé. The data sheet summarizes your education, experience, and accomplishments in a single document. Preparing such a data sheet enables you to adapt your qualifications for different career opportunities.

A good resumé data sheet forces you to think about all the important aspects of your background, and helps you to determine which of your experiences are most appropriate for each job you may decide to pursue. You should work with this form before writing a draft of your resumé. Table 2 shows a sample of a blank resumé data sheet.

Developing a Rough Draft Of Your Resumé

The rough draft stage transforms the skills and experiences that you identified in the resumé data sheet into a working document, which will resemble your final resumé in format. The basic differences between the rough draft of a resumé and the final one are that the rough draft can have grammatical and spelling errors and unpolished job descriptions, can be used to test out different layouts and type fonts, and can be produced on low-quality paper and printed in draft mode on a dot-matrix printer. In comparison, the final copy should have no errors, be attractively designed, be on high-quality paper, and be produced on a laser printer.

The rough draft should be shown to the college placement office, professors, and professionals in the field you wish to enter. Changes can be made on this document rather easily.

When preparing the rough draft, you should:

1. Prepare several alternatives. Experiment with different layouts and type fonts.
2. Ask several people to critically review the drafts. Accept the criticism. Make corrections as noted by your "reviewers." You should incorporate the best attributes of each draft in your final resumé.
3. Prepare your rough draft on a PC, if possible. This will allow you to make corrections and to give a diskette of the final version to a printer. Confirm that the company can use the word-processing program that you have used.
4. If you live on campus, make sure that you indicate both home and school addresses and telephone numbers on your

Table 2

Example of a Resumé Data Sheet

Name:
Address:
City/State:
Telephone:
[Provide multiple addresses and phone numbers where relevant. Indicate applicable dates for each address.]

Career Objective: [Indicate objective in broad terms so as not to the reduce chance of an interview.]

Educational Data: [List degrees in reverse chronological order. Show major, dates attended, overall average (if high), and average in major (if high). If you attended more than one college, name all colleges in reverse chronological order.]

Special Qualifications: [Briefly describe your special qualifications, relevant to your job objective. This may include a brief listing of relevant courses you have completed, fluency in a foreign language (if applicable), and special computer skills--such as Lotus 1-2-3 proficiency.]

Job Experiences: [List jobs in reverse chronological order. For each, show employer, dates employed, hours per week, job functions and responsibilities, special tasks, and special accomplishments--such as promotions and awards.]

Extracurricular Activities: [List key activities in reverse chronological order. For each, cite the organization, dates of participation, positions held, nature of responsibilities, and special accomplishments. Describe the organizations by using such terms as social fraternity, school service club, student counseling organization, or college newspaper.]

Honors: [Include key honors and awards in reverse chronological order. Show honors and awards such as making the Dean's list, service awards, and scholarships.]

Personal: [Use this section to include hobbies, special interests, and foreign travel. Tailor the section to the position sought. If you have worked while in college, you may wish to indicate the per cent of tuition earned.]

References: [It is customary to state that references will be supplied upon request. However, write up your references, particularly nonrelatives with important job titles, on your data sheet so that you can provide them when asked to do so.]

---

resumé. This will ensure that a potential employer can contact you in the event that he or she wants to call you when school is not in session. Be sure your answering machine is functioning properly and that the machine has an appropriate message.
5. Contact the references you list by name on your resumé in advance. Tell them your career plans, ask permission to use them as references, and ask them to notify you if they are called by a prospective employer. Confirm the working hours, job responsibilities, accomplishments, and reasons for leaving prior positions with past supervisors. Keep references informed as to your progress.

Arranging for the Final Copy of Your Resumé to Be Printed

After you have received the input of your reviewers and incorporated their suggestions, you are ready for the final copy of your resumé to be printed. In arranging for this,

1. Comparison shop among several reputable printers. When you check prices, verify the quality of paper, promised delivery times, and the types of fonts to be used.
2. Use a high-quality, watermarked paper and buy the matching envelopes. Purchase additional matching stationery for your cover letter. Use white or off-white stationery with black or blue ink.
3. Anticipate the quantity desired in advance of visiting the printer. Order ample quantities of your resumé. You will find that doubling the initial quantity may cost much less than placing two separate orders.
4. If you have multiple job objectives, consider having multiple resumés. You may want to tailor a different resumé to a specific job objective.
5. Have the printer show you one copy of the resumé before the balance are printed. Check this copy very carefully.

See Figure 1 for a sample resumé. Please note: After you have acquired substantial full-time work experience, that section will move ahead of the material on your education on your resumé. At that point, you will be marketing your employment background and using your education as complementary (not as primary).

Preparing the Cover Letter

Use a specially prepared cover letter to accompany each resumé that you send out. A good cover letter should be personally addressed and specify the job or kind of job for which you are applying. It will also describe why your skills and interests

Figure 1: A Sample Marketing Resumé

GEORGE LOUIS FLORES

Current Address	**Home Address**
155 Dryden Road	2000 Hampton Way
Ithaca, NY 14850	Oliver, NY 11566
(607) 555-1111	(516) 555-5555

OBJECTIVE

A position in media planning with a major advertising agency or advertiser. Formal training program desired.

EDUCATION

Ithaca College, Ithaca, NY, Bachelor of Science, June 1993
   Major: Marketing   Cumulative GPA: 3.2
   Minor: Psychology   Major GPA: 3.5

RELATED COURSES

Marketing, Mass Media, Theories of Communication, Marketing Research, Principles of Advertising, Intermediate Statistics

WORK EXPERIENCE

Student Intern, Haines & Gatsby Inc., Ithaca, NY, Spring 1993
   Worked in media research department for 20 hours per week.

Research Assistant, Professor Richard Wall, Marketing Department, Ithaca College, 1991-1992
   Organized data and research files, researched and photocopied relevant articles for research projects.

SPECIAL SKILLS

Good knowledge of French; Lotus 1-2-3; WordPerfect

EXTRACURRICULAR ACTIVITIES

Vice-President, American Marketing Association
Ithaca College Student Chapter, 1992-1993

HONORS

Dean's List, every semester

REFERENCES FURNISHED UPON REQUEST

are a good match for the company, and it will demonstrate that you know something about the firm (i.e., Why are you applying to this company for a position?). Although cover letters for different firms can have common components, they should also have elements that are tailored to each firm.

The cover letter should thank the addressee for his or her time and consideration. It should also say that you are looking forward to hearing from the firm or that you will contact the addressee at a later time.

Because cover letters should be individually prepared, you will need a good typewriter or access to a computer and high-quality printer. All envelopes should be typed.

Resumé Follow-Up

The last stage of the resumé process is the follow-up. It may be necessary for you to contact the company to determine your status. Although some potential employers will write to you within two to three weeks of receiving your cover letter and resumé, others will not.

If you do not hear from a potential employer, take the initiative and write or to call to ask about your standing. When doing this, be sure that you are professional and restate your strong interest in the company.

THE INTERVIEW PROCESS

One hundred resumés and cover letters may result in less than a handful of interviews, yet some students do not give sufficient attention to the interview process.

Below, the three major phases of the interview process are presented: planning for the interview, the interview, and the interview follow-up.

Planning for the Interview

Prior to any interview, you should carefully study the company and the industry in which it operates. You should also keep up to date on recent events involving the firm.

Your preparation may entail reviewing the company's annual report and reading relevant materials in your college library or placement office. At the very least, you should have a good understanding of the firm's line of business, current sales, sales growth, competitors, and industry trends.

If you are unsure as to how to get to the interview site (if it is off-campus), get careful directions and plan to get there quite early, to be on the safe side. Even when you are certain about how to get to an interview, always allow suffi-

cient time. Keep in mind that there may be some difficulty with traffic and/or parking. It is better to be at an interview a half hour early than to arrive a few minutes late.
Here are some other hints in preparing for an interview:

1. Dress conservatively. You are better off dressing too conservatively than too flashily, unless you are applying for a fashion-oriented position.
2. Bring a pad and several pens. Be prepared to write down important information you learned during the interview (but not during the interview itself).
3. Bring an additional copy of your resumé. Also bring a copy of your transcript, in case it is requested.
4. Try to not schedule more than two interviews per day. The interviewing process is stressful and most people perform best when interviews are spaced out.
5. Because people rarely perform at their best during early interviews, you should take as many interviews on campus as possible to get practice. You also should schedule the interview with your most desired employer after you have gained practice in being interviewed. But remember, when you take an on-campus interview, you are influencing an employer's perceptions toward your whole school. Therefore, prepare well for these interviews and treat them seriously.

Try to anticipate questions that are commonly asked by interviewers and think about possible answers. Here are some popular questions, in no particular order:

. Why are you interested in our firm?
. What is your career objective?
. Do you view yourself as a leader or a follower? Why?
. Why did you decide to major in marketing?
. Do your college grades accurately reflect your motivation and/or ability? Why or why not?
. Tell me about your experiences at college over the past four years.
. Tell me about your work experience over the past four years.
. What per cent of your college tuition did you earn while a student?
. Which college courses did you like the most? The least? Why?
. What are your plans for graduate school?
. What position would you want to have in our company in three years? In five years?
. Are you willing to relocate?
. What are your special abilities relative to a career with this firm?
. Describe your personality.
. What is your greatest strength? Your greatest weakness?
. What did you do in the last month that gave you the most

. enjoyment? The least enjoyment? Why?
. One-hundred people have applied for this job, why should we select you?
. What two questions would you like to ask me about our firm?

Review each of these questions. Write down appropriate responses. After you have written down your thoughts, reflect on them. You may also wish to role play answers with a good friend, your parents, or a professor. However, do not memorize answers because this may cause you to lose some of your spontaneity in the actual interview.

During the Interview

When taking an interview, listen to the interviewer, be poised and self-confident (but not cocky), demonstrate a very sincere interest in the firm, and show that you understand company and industry dynamics.
Some specific hints for the interview are:

. Always be polite and never get rattled. Try to be as relaxed as the situation will allow.
. Use the interviewer's name. Refer to the person as Mr. or Ms. _____, not by his or her first name, unless otherwise instructed.
. Listen carefully to all questions. If you are unsure of the question, ask the interviewer to repeat it.
. Be sure to answer the questions actually asked by the interviewer.
. Show that you have prepared for the interview by including facts you have learned in your answers.
. If asked about special abilities, such as computer skills or foreign language competency, be accurate. For example, if you are competent in reading, but only fair in speaking a foreign language, then state this.
. Be honest about the reasons for leaving other jobs.
. Do not speak ill of past supervisors or jobs.
. Acknowledge your past accomplishments, but put them into perspective. For example, if you were responsible for a successful fund-raising drive organized by your fraternity or your sorority, note that the success was also due to other highly motivated volunteers.
. You can think for 15-20 seconds before answering a complex question.
. Ask your own questions, such as: What are you looking for in an ideal candidate? What is the usual career path for someone like myself in your firm? How long does a typical person stay at each stage in that path? Could you please tell me about the firm's formal and informal training programs? If I am offered a position, would I be expected to relocate? If

yes, to where? What is the company's policy with regard to tuition remission for an MBA degree? What are the next steps in your company's screening process? When will I be hearing from you?

Take mental notes. Write down your thoughts right after the interview, once you have left the room. Figure 2 presents a sample post-interview note-taking form.

The Interview Follow-Up

After an interview, it is customary to write a thank you letter to the interviewer. Although the letter should be brief, it should thank the interviewer for his or her time and the information shared with you. If you remain interested in the position, you should convey your feelings. However, a thank you letter should be written even if you no longer have an interest in the job. A sample thank you letter is contained in Figure 3.

It is also acceptable to contact the firm by either phone or letter if you have not been contacted within the time frame stated by the interviewer.

Be ethical in your dealings. If you are given an offer and are undecided about whether to accept, then ask for a few days or a week to reply--while still conveying your enthusiasm with regard to the offer. Tell a firm that you are interested or that you are not interested in accepting an offer as soon as you have definitely decided. Do not put undue pressure on a firm to make a decision on you or attempt to drive a hard bargain by pitting one company's offer against another. Once you accept a job, do not consider other offers or take additional interviews. As previously noted, your job search behavior will not only affect you but current and future classmates at your college. Please don't do something that will cause a firm to think less of your school or to stop recruiting there.

THE FORMAT OF THIS BOOK

In the following chapters of this career guide, these topics will be covered:

. Career opportunities in marketing (Chapter Two)
. Marketing-related jobs and internships during college (Chapter Three)
. Companies regularly seeking college graduates for marketing-related positions (Chapter Four)
. Professional and trade associations in marketing-related fields (Chapter Five)

GOOD LUCK!

Figure 2

A Sample Post-Interview Note-Taking Form

==

Name, address, and phone number of company:

Date, time, place, and length of interview:

Interviewer's name:

Overall impression of company:

Overall impression of how the interview went:

What type of job is available? What do I think about it?

What are the prospects for advancement at the firm?

Other key points to keep in mind:

Do I remain interested in a position with this firm?

If yes, when should I follow-up?

What should I improve on in future interviews?

==

Figure 3

A Sample Thank You Letter

GEORGE LOUIS FLORES

Current Address	**Home Address**
155 Dryden Road	2000 Hampton Way
Ithaca, NY 14850	Oliver, NY 11566
(607) 555-1111	(516) 555-5555

April 30, 1993

Ms. Lisa Brown
Campus Coordinator
J. Walter Saatchi Company
North Michigan Avenue
Chicago, IL 60611

Dear Ms. Brown:

I much enjoyed my interview with the J. Walter Saatchi Company last week.

Your one-year training program seems very exciting to me. Also, because I studied marketing research at Ithaca College and used and evaluated a number of Lotus 1-2-3 templates in my advertising class, I was particularly impressed with the degree of computerization at your firm.

The interview has convinced me that media planning is the right field for me and that J. Walter Saatchi is the firm with which I would most like to work.

Thank you for your time and your kind comments about my accomplishments at Ithaca College.

Sincerely,

George Louis Flores

CHAPTER TWO

CAREER OPPORTUNITIES IN MARKETING

OVERVIEW[1]

The basic goal of most firms is to market their goods or services profitably. In small firms, all marketing responsibilities may be assumed by the owner or chief executive officer. In large firms, which may offer numerous goods and services nationally or even worldwide, experienced marketing, product, distribution, sales, advertising, public relations, and pricing managers often coordinate these and related activities.

In large firms, the executive vice-president for marketing typically directs the overall marketing strategy--including market planning, marketing research, product development, distribution, advertising, public relations, personal selling, sales promotion, pricing, and other activities. These functions are supervised by middle and supervisory managers who oversee staffs of professionals and technicians.

Marketing managers develop the firm's detailed marketing strategy. With the help of subordinates, they determine the demand for the goods and services offered by the firm and its competitors and identify potential consumers--like industrial firms, wholesalers, retailers, government, or the general public. Markets are further categorized according to such factors as region, age, income, and life-style.

Specialized managers in bigger firms also develop product, distribution, and price strategies--with an eye to introducing exciting new products, maintaining the success of the firm's mature products, gaining dealer acceptance and cooperation, optimizing the firm's share of the market, and getting satisfactory profits. Marketing managers are very tuned in to the actions of the marketplace and competitors. In collaboration with other executives, they monitor the trends that indicate a need for new goods and services and oversee product development. When a firm assumes multiple channel functions--such as manufacturing, wholesaling, and retailing--separate managers are required for each level of the distribution channel.

Sales managers direct a firm's sales program. They assign territories and establish training programs for their sales representatives. These managers advise the representatives on ways to improve sales performance. In large firms, they oversee regional and local sales managers and their staffs, and maintain contact with dealers and distributors. They analyze statistics gathered by their staffs to determine sales potential and inventory requirements and to monitor the preferences

---

1 The material in this section is adapted by the authors from *Occupational Outlook Handbook*, 1992-93 Edition (Washington, D.C.: U.S. Department of Labor, May 1992), pp. 48-50.

of customers. Such information is vital to develop products and maximize profits.

Except in the largest firms, advertising and promotion staffs are usually small and serve as a liaison between a firm and an outside agency to which many advertising or promotional functions are contracted. Advertising managers oversee account services, creative services, and media services departments. Promotion managers direct promotion programs, which combine advertising with purchase incentives to increase sales of goods or services.

Public relations managers direct publicity programs to a targeted public, using any necessary communication media, designed to maintain the support of the specific group upon whom their firms' success depends, such as consumers, stockholders, or the general public. For example, public relations managers may justify a firm's point of view on health or environmental issues to community or special interest groups.

Table 1 lists just some of the many positions available for those who are interested in a career in marketing.

A wide range of educational backgrounds is suitable for entry into marketing-related jobs. Some employers prefer a bachelor's or master's degree in business administration with an emphasis on marketing. Courses in business law, economics, accounting, finance, mathematics, and statistics are also recommended. In technical industries, such as computer and electronics manufacturing, a bachelor's degree in engineering or science combined with a master's degree in business administration may be preferred. For advertising management, some employers prefer a bachelor's degree in advertising or journalism; the curriculum should include courses in marketing, consumer behavior, marketing research, sales, communications methods and technology, and visual arts--such as art history and photography. Other employers prefer a broad liberal arts background--with a bachelor's degree in sociology, psychology, literature, or philosophy, among other subjects. However, requirements vary depending upon the particular job.

For all specialties, courses in basic marketing and management and completion of an internship or the acquisition of meaningful work experience while in school are recommended. Familiarity with word processing and data-base applications is also important for many marketing-related positions.

Most middle- and upper-level marketing positions are filled by promoting experienced staff or related professional or technical personnel--for example, sales representatives, purchasing agents, buyers, product specialists, distribution specialists, advertising specialists, and public relations specialists. In small firms, where the number of positions is limited, advancement to a management position may come slowly. In large firms, promotion may occur more quickly.

Although a person's experience, ability, and leadership are emphasized for promotion, advancement may be accelerated

Table 1

The Variety of Marketing Positions That Are Available
(A Selected Listing)

Account manager
Advertising copywriter
Advertising layout person
Advertising manager
Advertising production
  manager
Advertising research
  director
Agent (broker)
Catalog manager
Commercial artist
Consumer affairs
  (customer relations)
  specialist
Credit manager
Customer service
  representative
Direct-to-home (or office)
  salesperson
Display worker
Fashion designer
Franchisee
Franchisor
Freight forwarder
Industrial designer
Industrial traffic manager
International marketer
Inventory manager
Life insurance agent
  (broker)
Manufacturers'
  representative
Marketing manager (vice-
  president)

Marketing research project
  supervisor
Media director (space or
  time buyer)
Media planner
Missionary salesperson
Order-fulfillment
  manager
Packaging specialist
Political consultant
Pricing economist
Product manager (brand
  manager)
Property and casualty
  insurance agent (broker)
Public relations director
Purchasing agent
Real-estate agent
  (broker)
Retail buyer
Retail department manager
Retail merchandise
  manager
Retail salesperson
Retail store manager
Sales engineer
Sales manager
Sales promotion director
Salesperson
Securities salesperson
  (commodities broker)
Traffic manager
Warehouser
Wholesale salesperson

SOURCE: Adapted from Joel R. Evans and Barry Berman, *Market-
    ing*, Fifth Edition (New York: Macmillan, 1992), pp.
    A2-A3.

by participation in the management training programs conducted by large firms. In addition, marketing and other associations, often in collaboration with colleges and universities, sponsor national or local training programs. Firms often pay all or part of the cost for those who successfully complete courses.

Those interested in marketing careers should be mature, creative, motivated, resistant to stress, and flexible, yet decisive. The ability to communicate persuasively, orally and in writing, is vital. Marketing personnel also need tact, good judgment, and the ability to establish effective relationships with supervisory and professional staff members and clients.

Because of the importance and high visibility of their jobs, marketing personnel are often prime candidates for advancement. Well-trained, experienced, successful people may be promoted to higher positions in their own or other firms. Some become top executives. Marketing managers with extensive experience and sufficient capital may open their businesses.

The employment of marketing personnel is expected to increase much faster than the average for all occupations through the year 2005. Increasingly intense domestic and foreign competition in the goods and services offered to consumers should require greater marketing efforts. In addition to much faster than average growth, many job openings will occur each year to replace people who move into top management positions, transfer to other jobs, or leave the labor force. However, many highly coveted jobs will be sought by other managers or experienced professional and technical personnel, resulting in substantial job competition. College graduates with extensive experience, creativity, and strong communication skills should have the best job opportunities.

To give you a better feel for the kinds of marketing-related career opportunities that exist, the next several sections will describe some of the career options in advertising, logistics, sales, and wholesaling and retailing. Please note that these career options represent only the tip of the iceberg (as you can see when looking again at Table 1).

ADVERTISING CAREERS[2]

What Is Advertising?

It's a thumping, throbbing, visually spectacular television commercial. It's three lines of copy in the classifieds about

2 The material in this section is adapted by the authors from *Go For It: A Guide to Careers in Advertising* (New York: American Association of Advertising Agencies). Reprinted by permission.

a used car. It's a funny radio spot, an eight-piece, embossed invitation to a magazine subscription, and a fabulous contest. It calls attention to soft drinks, detergents, the United Fund, cancer research, and stereo equipment.

It cries; it laughs; it sings a song. It's beautiful, or it's startling, or it's coolly business-like. Sometimes, when poorly conceived, or carelessly produced, it can be crass or naive. But when it is at its best, it is tremendous.

Advertising can be entertaining, but is more than entertainment. Advertising is an indispensable part of our economic system. It is the vital link between businesses and consumers.

It informs; it reminds; it introduces. It gives a good or service a personality, and makes it friendly and familiar. It delineates differences, defines benefits and advantages. It makes better-informed and more discerning customers--the foundation of a free, competitive society.

To put it simply, advertising is salesmanship. It can make the difference between business success and failure. It is a cost-efficient way of telling buyers what is for sale and why they should buy it. At the very least, it seeks to persuade someone who is in the market for a given good or service to consider a particular brand.

The business of advertising involves marketing goals and artistic ingenuity. It applies quantitative and qualitative research to the creative process. It is the marriage of analysis and imagination, of marketing professional and artist.

Advertising is art and science, show business, and just plain business, rolled into one. And it employs some of the brightest and most creative economists, researchers, artists, producers, writers, and businesspeople in the world today.

All good advertising includes some basic steps before it appears in public: It defines its market: new parents for disposable diapers; women for lipstick. It assesses the competition: how much money is being spent on television ads; what creative approach is being used. It determines who the target audience is, and how and why it chooses the products it does: the convenience of a detergent with built-in softener; the capacity of a minivan. It sets goals and a budget: what the advertising should achieve and how much must be spent to achieve those goals. It determines the media: what vehicle (television, newspapers, magazines) will best reach the target audience; to be effective, how frequently the message should be seen. It creates a message: what pictures, words, and music will best attract and appeal to the specific target audience.

An advertiser can take these steps by itself or hire an outside company to do them. The outside company is usually an advertising agency, an entity specializing in the business of advertising. It helps the advertising firms (its clients) to identity prospective customers, create the advertising, and buy broadcast (television, radio) time and print (magazine, newspaper) space to carry the advertising.

Jobs in an Advertising Agency

Agencies handle a broad range of marketing tasks that require people with experience and ability in overall management and specialized fields. In a small agency, one person may wear several hats (e.g., media planner and buyer), while at a large agency some people will tend to specialize (e.g., network television buyer). However, in all agencies, jobs usually fall into five categories: account management, creative, media, market research, and support services and administration.

Account Management

At an agency, the client and its business are usually called "the account." One advertiser may offer many products and ask separate agencies to handle each one. Another may use a single agency to handle several products. Whatever the particular situation, the account management department is where the resources of the agency and the needs of the client connect.

The account manager oversees the advertising business that has been assigned to the agency, and is ultimately responsible for the quality of service the client receives. The account manager is the client's representative at the agency and the agency's representative to the client. It is his or her job to get the client its money's worth, but at a profitable return for the agency. This means knowing how to handle people at the agency so they give a client their best effort without spending more time than the income from a client justifies.

An effective account manager develops a thorough knowledge of the client's business, the consumer, the marketplace, and all aspects of advertising. As a team leader and strategist, this person must communicate the client's needs clearly to the agency team, plan effectively to maximize staff time and energy, and present the agency's recommendations candidly to the client. He or she must know all about the agency: who are the most qualified people in each department, and how to get their attention when needed. An account manager must also know all about the client, learning every aspect of the client's business--ideally, from product development through the entire marketing operation--well enough to command a client's respect when presenting the agency's recommendations.

The major entry-level position is the assistant account executive (manager). A typical assistant reports to an account executive and has a wide range of responsibilities. Some common duties include reporting client billing and forecasting agency income, analyzing competitive activity and consumer trends, writing reports from meetings, and coordinating creative, media, research, and production projects.

Successful candidates have strong general business skills: the ability to write and speak well, leadership experience, a capacity for statistical analysis, and organizational skills. In addition, these traits are important: working well under pressure, handling several tasks simultaneously, coordinating the work and energy of diverse types of people, creative sensibility, and an interest in advertising and marketing. Candidates should have a bachelor's degree and, in some cases, a master of business administration. A degree in advertising or marketing is not necessarily a prerequisite.

In the agency business, the account management and media departments hire the most entry-level candidates. Some large agencies have training programs.

An entry-level position usually leads to account executive and then to more senior positions, with responsibility for more than one account and for the work of several account executives. Ultimately, account management people can assume broader office and corporate positions. The largest percentage of top agency executives have come out of account management.

Creative

The creative department of an agency is responsible for developing the ideas, images, and words that make up commercials and ads. While many people in an agency contribute to this process, the invention and production of advertising is mainly the responsibility of copywriters and art directors.

When a copywriter and art director are given an account, they must learn about the product to be advertised, marketing strategy, consumer or potential consumer, media to be used, advertising by competitors, production budget, and client personnel with whom the agency deals. The research, account management, and media departments provide basic information on these topics. However, the creative people will most likely want to gain first-hand experience with the client's product.

After the creative people gain as much information as possible, they agree on a general direction. The art director and copywriter work as a team--trying ideas on each other, on the creative director, and then on the other agency groups working on the account. These executions are reviewed by senior members of the agency (including legal counsel), sometimes called the creative review board, to evaluate whether they match the goals of the marketing and advertising strategy.

Reviewed creative executions are presented to the client for approval. Once the client approves, the art director and copywriter work with print and broadcast production people to produce the final versions of the advertising.

Magazines and newspapers require camera-ready copy. To prepare such print advertisements, agencies rely upon outside services, from photographers to typesetters. Agency specialists in print production oversee this subcontracted work. TV stations require videotape; radio stations must have audio

MARKETING:
CAREERS
 IN
ADVERTISING
(READ SECTION
  ESPECIALLY
  PART ON
  "CREATIVE")

ials often involve a large cast of
ency producers oversee the completion
o commercials. They hire directors,
film crews, and actors. In addition,
et, work with composers and musicians,
eview and editing of the rough film or
version.
l position is the junior copywriter. A
er assists one or more copywriters in
ad copy, writing copy for established
vising sales promotion materials. With
might include generating ideas for
for TV commercials and radio ads.

A successful candidate will not only have outstanding writing skills but have a "love affair" with words and symbols and their use in communication. Interest in a wide range of subjects and an insatiable sense of curiosity are assets. Candidates should have some knowledge of marketing and how words and visuals have been used in advertising. Agencies expect job candidates to demonstrate their talent by showing portfolios of previous creative work, ideas, and "rough" designs of potential campaigns, even if they were done in a class. Most agencies look for candidates with proven intellectual ability and emotional maturity. Degrees in English, journalism, or advertising and marketing can be helpful. Some large firms have entry-level training programs in copywriting.

Media

The most innovative and creative advertising can fail if it's presented to the wrong audience, or if it's presented at the wrong time, or if it's presented in the wrong place. The media department is responsible for placing advertising where it will reach the right people at the right time and in the right place--and do so in a cost-effective way.

When working on a particular ad campaign, media planners discuss, with the client and other agency people, the goals of the marketing strategy as well as a description of the potential consumer. They think about the kinds of media the target group might read, listen to, or watch. They compare the content, image, and format of each medium with the nature of the product, its image, and the goals of the advertising campaign. It is the responsibility of the media department to develop a plan that answers the question: How can the greatest number of people in the target group be reached often enough to have a message seen and remembered--and, at the lowest possible cost?

Once a media plan has been developed, shown to a client, and approved, media buyers negotiate for space and time. Buyers must not only find and reserve available space and time, but also negotiate the best price. Will a station offer a better price if more time slots are bought? Will prime time be discounted if a buyer is willing to also purchase some less desirable time in the morning or late night?

After space and time have been purchased, the department must monitor the media to make sure the ads actually appeared, in the proper form and at the proper time as ordered. If a discrepancy occurs, the department negotiates an adjustment to the billing or accepts a credit for additional time or space.

A major entry-level position is the assistant media planner. A typical assistant works for a media planner and gathers and studies data on people's viewing and reading habits, compares editorial content and programming for various media, computes reach and frequency for specific target groups and campaigns, learns about media in general and media vehicles in particular (such as the *Wall Street Journal*), and becomes familiar with media data banks and information sources.

These tasks require the ability to find and analyze data, apply computer skills, ask innovative questions, and interpret or explain findings with attention to quantitative and qualitative considerations. A planner must gain knowledge of what information is important and where to find it. By assisting in gathering statistics to support a variety of plans, he or she becomes familiar with broad media characteristics and trends.

Another entry-level job is the assistant media buyer. This person reports to a media buyer and knows when and where space and time are available for purchase; reconciles media orders with what actually appears; calculates rates, usage, and budgets; learns terminology and operating procedures; develops skills in negotiation and communication with media sales representatives; and becomes familiar with the media market.

These tasks require ease at working with numbers, superior communications skills, and the ability to work under pressure. Skills in negotiation and sales are especially advantageous.

Successful media candidates must have very strong general business skills--the ability to write and speak effectively, developed organizational skills, aptitude for working with numbers and statistics, and basic computer skills. A degree in advertising or marketing is not necessarily a prerequisite.

An entry-level job usually leads to media planner or media buyer. In small agencies, these two jobs may be combined. It is usual for planners and buyers to have expertise in specific media categories. The next step is supervisory. A media planning supervisor coordinates the work of planners and presents recommendations to the account group and client. The broadcast buying supervisor oversees buying operations. With greater experience, media people advance to any of several positions-- associate media director, manager of media research, network supervisor, director of spot broadcast, group media director, director of programming and negotiations, and media director. Many agencies have top media people represented in senior management and as members on their boards of directors.

Market Research

The key role of a market research department is to understand the consumer's wants, desires, thoughts, concerns, motivating forces, and ideals. By studying secondary data, doing interviews, testing people's reactions to new ad copy, tracking sales volume, or studying buying trends, an advertising agency researcher becomes an expert on consumer behavior.

Most researchers are assigned to specific accounts and work as advisers to the account, creative, and media people. They help develop, refine, and evaluate potential strategies and are called upon to react to possible creative approaches based upon their understanding of the consumer. This might be done with the creative team during the process or with account managers as evaluators of creative alternatives. Some agencies employ researchers specializing in specific research areas.

The research department also oversees projects that are subcontracted to outside research firms. An example is surveys of shoppers at malls. Agency researchers design the questionnaire and interpret results, but a private firm conducts the interviews and summarizes the data so the researcher can write a report on the survey.

The major entry-level position is the assistant research executive. A typical assistant reports directly to a research executive. Duties usually include getting data from secondary sources, following the progress of research projects, assisting in the development of primary research tools, and learning to analyze facts and numbers, and explaining what they mean.

Successful candidates have strong quantitative skills and the aptitude for analyzing and interpreting qualitative as well as quantitative data. Computer literacy is advantageous. Candidates should be able to write and speak effectively, work well under pressure, and organize priorities. They should be interested in forecasting and human behavior. A bachelor's degree is the minimum requirement, but it is not unusual to find people who have master's or doctorate degrees in agency research departments. Employers are attracted to candidates whose majors are research-related. Some academic disciplines fitting this category are sociology, psychology, marketing, marketing research, economics, advertising, journalism, quantitative methods, anthropology, and mass communications. Entry-level positions are relatively rare in medium- and small-sized advertising agencies.

A job as an assistant research executive usually leads to a supervisory position involved with managing research on individual accounts or brands and overseeing the work of other assistants. The next step is managing a specialized research function or being responsible for all research on more than one account. A research person may have the opportunity to move into more general (higher-level) corporate management or marketing functions.

Support Services and Administration

Like any well-run business, an advertising agency must have a full complement of people who handle accounting, personnel, clerical, and office services. In addition, agency traffic managers make sure that, once started, an ad or commercial moves smoothly through the agency, additions and corrections are handled promptly and correctly, approvals are obtained, and the whole job arrives at the publication or the broadcast station on time. Cost controllers monitor agency costs, making sure that work stays within budget or that everyone is aware of, and approves, any needed changes in the budget.

Other agency employees may include lawyers, librarians, and certain specialists. For instance, agencies with big food or packaged-goods accounts may employ nutritionists and home economists. Those with health products or medical accounts may employ physicians. Diversity is one more aspect that makes agency work such a fascinating and rewarding career choice.

LOGISTICS CAREERS[3]

What Is Logistics?

The term may not be familiar to you, but the function is something from which you benefit every day. Logistics (or distribution) is the term describing the various functions related to the movement of an item from the place where it was made or grown to the place where it is used or consumed. For example, because of the logistics/distribution process, there is fresh food in your local grocery store, regardless of the season.

All of the activities involved in moving products to the right places at the right times (as opposed to making them) can be termed "logistics" or "distribution." The act of supervising or managing this far-reaching activity is generally known as "logistics management" or "distribution management." Those persons who work in this industry are generally referred to as "logistics managers" or "distribution managers."

The components of a typical logistics system are: customer service, demand forecasting, distribution communications, inventory control, material handling, order processing, parts and service support, plant and warehouse site selection (location analysis), purchasing, packaging, return goods handling, salvage and scrap disposal, traffic and transportation, and warehousing and storage. A job in a small firm may involve all

3 The material in this section is adapted by the authors from *Careers in Logistics* (Oak Brook, IL: Council of Logistics Management). Reprinted by permission.

of these, while working for a large company may mean involvement with only one or a few areas. Sometimes, logistics managers may have responsibilities going beyond this list.

What Background Do You Need to Enter the Field of Logistics?

Most certainly, the first thing you will need to enter the field of logistics management is a college degree. Whereas at one time it was perfectly acceptable to learn through on-the-job training, those days are past. A college degree is increasingly expected and necessary for upward mobility. One poll of the Council of Logistics Management membership indicated that well over 80 per cent of logistics managers hold at least a bachelor's degree. Graduate level work is not yet a requirement, but it is both valued and rewarded. Recent studies at Ohio State University show that persons with advanced degrees are more likely to receive higher salaries and higher level positions. This is particularly true in the technical and quantitative areas--logistics planning and analysis and systems design and control.

It is most important for you to obtain a good business administration background. Increasing numbers of colleges and universities now offer complete majors in logistics and physical distribution. Other major areas of value include management, marketing, operations, traffic management, computer science, and statistics/quantitative theory. Also valuable in rounding out your background are cost accounting, business law, economics, human relations/personnel, and communications. People skills are very important in this field, and it is essential that you learn to speak and write effectively.

Summer or part-time work and internship programs are often available in logistics. These will give you a chance for practical experience and can serve to confirm that your interests and goals match well with the field of logistics management. The time for career planning is NOT after graduation.

Jobs in Logistics

Following are a series of interviews with people working in logistics. Each one will tell you how they began their career, describe current positions and responsibilities, what they like (and don't like) about their jobs, and then offer advice and suggestions for your own career in logistics management.

Inventory Control Manager

"I was a marketing major in college. After graduation, I worked first as a marketing analyst and from there I moved into inventory.

"Presently, I am the vice-president of inventory management and report directly to the president. Reporting to me are inventory coordinators, inventory controllers, and inventory managers for each product type. The department is divided into two parts: the basic responsibility is to make sure that all of our stock-keeping units are in adequate supply--both components and finished goods. We work very closely with design and preproduction so that production can be contracted out. Also, we are responsible for the overall quality of the product. The objectives of this position are to maximize customer service levels, inventory investment, and manufacturing efficiencies.

"On an average day, one of the major things I do is look at computer reports--just to get an overview and to see where we are--and follow through with actions as required. I spend a considerable amount of time evaluating reports on suppliers. Then, of course, other parts of my days are spent in writing, attending meetings, traveling, and planning. About 45 to 50 hours per week are spent on the job. I do some work at home-- correspondence and special reports.

"I probably have the most interesting job in the world. 'Perfect inventory' really is an unattainable goal but I feel that striving and getting close are very rewarding. It's a constant challenge and the politics are difficult. Deadlines make the job stressful, as does change, but I love it.

"For this position, you need a whole lot of patience and the ability to get along with people. Treating people fairly is very important--as is the ability to really listen. Computer skills would really be an asset. Communication is quite important. Besides the technical skills in your own field of interest, financial ability is very important and I would advise concentrating on finance, economics, and marketing.

"Students interested in this area should consider examining all schools that have a formal inventory program. A summer job in warehousing or production would be very helpful. Join one of the professional organizations. And once you're out of college, I believe the best training you can get is to work for a large corporation."

Warehousing/Operations Manager

"I am a vice-president of warehousing operations for a major U.S. food company. I am responsible for all activities in the warehouse that are outside the office area, including receiving, storing, and shipping merchandise.

"My basic mission is to determine and develop the logistics strategies and practices that will support our corporate objective. My major responsibilities are identifying areas within the company that offer some opportunity for improvement; optimizing our investment in all of our locations--in inventory, facilities, and people; and matching the corporate distribution support capabilities to the outlying marketing, business, and operational needs.

"I am in the office by 7:15 A.M. and leave between 6:00 and 6:30 at night; so I spend about 50 hours a week on the job. It is not only planning which consumes a considerable amount of time, but also monitoring various activities and projects. Besides that, we do some entertaining of customers, which often involves evenings and weekends.

"There are very few average days in warehousing. Normally on Mondays, I get caught up on the paperwork from the previous week and I make a plan for the coming week. About 40 per cent of my time is spent in planning for the future. Another 40 per cent is spent on operational activities, and the final 20 per cent on people-/personnel-related activities.

"What I like best about my job is that it's never dull. Just when I think I've seen or heard it all, something happens to prove I haven't. I have a lot of opportunity to work for the good of my company and to improve our status. The position involves coordinating the efforts of a lot of people so that the transition of our products from the time of production through their final disposition to the customer happens in the least amount of time and with the lowest costs possible. This job is competitive, but the very fact that it is competitive makes for an average day when there's never enough time to do what I want to do. It gives me a chance to use my head. I enjoy the challenge of identifying what appears to be a problem and solving it. I get satisfaction from preventing everyday problems and coming up with different ways to prevent them in the future. It is all done through people.

"My people do all the labor negotiations with the various unions that are involved with us, all the office administration, and the related data processing. They also do pricing. Other significant concerns include sanitary conditions of the facility, service, and the ability to consolidate merchandise.

"Generalizing about warehousing and the place it occupies on the organizational chart is difficult. Warehousing might be found in a logistics group or as part of a customer distribution and services group or as a separate entity. In my firm, our domestic organization is centralized. It has four principal groups, including transportation and field operations.

"I began working in logistics when I was 20 years old. When I took the job in the warehouse, I had no intention of staying. I didn't plan for it--I just happened into it. That was fifteen years ago. With the competition for jobs the way it is today, fewer people just luck into a job anymore. It takes planning and preparation. Today, most new hires join the firm through the estimating and planning organization or via our distribution systems organization. However, even our college graduates spend time in the warehouse. From there, they might move into a supervisory position for their first taste of management. The next move could involve them in wide-ranging operations activities, such as planning and organization. The final step would be a job at corporate headquarters.

"Of all the skills necessary for success, organization is a must. Other definite assets are the ability to handle people and to solve problems. Considering that most of logistics is unionized, it would be good to pick up something in college that would provide a basic knowledge of dealing with labor and negotiating. You don't have to know how to program a computer, but you will need to know the computer well enough to understand your involvement with it—as well as how it interfaces with other people—so that you will be able to spot a systems problem and what could be the cause of it.

"I think that a financial background is extremely helpful, being able to evaluate projects and allocate resources. It is useful to have a systems orientation and know how to set up a project. I think it is good to have a basic understanding of sales forecasting and how to evaluate statistical data to comprehend the total inventory management process. There are some aspects of transportation that are helpful to any manager."

Administrative Manager

"I started in logistics management by working in a warehouse—loading box cars and trucks on a summer job while I was still in college. Soon after, I changed my major to transportation and traffic management. I began in an office position as an assistant superintendent and then transferred to another location as superintendent. From there, I moved into the distribution division at our world headquarters.

"As regional manager of administration, I supervise an organization of 300 people with two subordinate managers. This includes personnel, equipment, materials, facilities, product handling, inventory control, building services, customer relations, order processing, office services, and district operations. My primary goal is to provide maximum support to all divisions via the regional or district distribution centers and to ensure that timely, cost-effective service is provided to those units and their customers. Additionally, I may be called on to represent other corporate divisions within a regional area. Basically then, our role is to motivate our various divisions (warehousing, data processing, and transportation) to improve their operations by using better facilities, intracoordinating operations, and improving their order processing, inventory control, and scheduling systems.

"I don't know if I have a routine or 'typical' day. Probably 20 per cent of my day is spent on administrative matters, and the rest of my time consists of reviewing the status of various projects with either my staff or my boss. We are continually setting target dates and evaluating how effective we are in meeting our goals. A certain amount of every day is spent handling written and phone correspondence. I spent last week integrating the annual personnel review and evaluation of my staff. Generally, I spend 10 hours a day, five days a week on my job. Fifty per cent of my time is spent traveling.

"This is a very challenging career field. No two days are alike and there are tremendous opportunities for creativity. Nonfinancial rewards are great because we are so closely related to the sales process that I see the results quickly. I like dealing with people and the sense of accomplishment that I feel after arriving at viable solutions to a problem.

"Some employees begin in a training program where they are exposed to production, marketing, and line and corporate staff operations. Others begin in sales, working for a terminal manager. Personality, energy level, drive, and enthusiasm are the important attributes in a job candidate. One of the primary requirements is a college degree in the business field. While a specialty in systems or transportation can be very helpful, even more important is a broad business education. Essential skills are an ability to manage people, an understanding of budget and finance, and an analytical intellect capable of quickly assessing a situation and organizing priorities. Flexibility is also very important, as is knowledge of computers.

"I would advise anyone interested in logistics management to get a college degree with a general management background and a focus on physical distribution, logistics, or traffic. It would be desirable to include computer courses, especially an overview of management information systems. And be certain to learn how to communicate effectively."

Transportation Manager

"My college major was general business with extra courses in statistics, finance, and accounting. My first position after graduation was traffic coordinator and from there I became traffic manager.

"Currently, I am an associate director of logistics in corporate transportation, which means I am involved in all aspects of transportation for the corporation. This includes inbound, between facilities, and outbound. There are five functional areas for which I am responsible: transportation operations, transportation and rate analysis, transportation planning and control, transportation administration, and traffic services. Additionally, I work closely with the purchasing, international, marketing, and sales divisions.

"Overall, my primary responsibilities include: supervising the various functions and personnel; negotiating rates with warehousing and transportation firms; planning, monitoring, and implementing the distribution department's budget; establishing the most beneficial routing of company shipments for satisfactory customer service; determining pricing levels; and planning--on a quarterly, a yearly, and a five-year horizon.

"If you consider today as one of my 'typical' days, my schedule includes negotiating for LTL (less-than-truckload) commodities, checking on the status of an air-freight claim, implementing a plant distribution survey, training personnel about customs forms, and detailing a changeover from truck to rail for one of our larger customers. I'm also working on my production schedule and the fiscal budget, and I'm attending a Trucking Association luncheon. I usually work about 10 hours a day, but travel time and after-hours meetings often bring the total hours worked closer to 60 per week.

"I love the excitement of something new each day and the sense of accomplishment. I also enjoy the interfacing with each of the different company divisions and the opportunity to work with many different firms outside the organization. Additionally, I like the authority in this position--in terms of staff, material resources, and budget--and my compensation.

"I believe one of the most important skills necessary for this job is adaptability--everything is in a constant state of change. And of course a basic understanding of transportation is essential. It's not just knowing different transportation modes; it's understanding how transportation affects all the other areas of the company. Knowledge of the computer, electronic data processing, customer service, inventory control, and production scheduling is very helpful. The ability to communicate is important--listening, speaking, writing, and other nonverbal communication. Other attributes include the ability to plan, control, influence, motivate, lead, organize, select employees, and administer. It is more important than ever to know how to handle things from a resources standpoint.

"My advice to anyone interested in a transportation career is to get a broad background, as well as traditional transportation courses. Get entry-level experience prior to graduation and learn the jargon before looking for that first job."

Customer Service Manager

"I grew up in a family that was in the motor carrier business, so I have always been intimately involved with and aware of the logistics industry. After college and graduate school, I accepted a job in customer service with a major pharmaceutical firm. Now, I am a customer service supervisor. Reporting to me are the order entry and customer service departments. My manager is the customer service director.

"I enjoy being a customer service supervisor and having the responsibility for making sure that shipments take place as scheduled. I function as the liaison between customers and the sales force. In this job, I rarely encounter the mundane. More than 60 per cent of my time is spent in an administrative capacity, such as reviewing performance standards. About 10 to 15 per cent is devoted to personnel matters--such as training, performance reviews, and the allocation of responsibilities. The other 30 per cent is spent actually working in customer service. I normally work about 50 hours per week. Travel is minimal and I rarely find it necessary to work at home.

"One delight about this business is being involved with so many different people and businesses. It is quite rewarding to experience the variety of types of organizations, methods of production, marketing schemes, and people. Changing relationships with people, positions, attitudes, and philosophies is a continual learning process--and again, a rewarding one. The amount of paperwork we process can be frustrating. And this, as well as administrative responsibilities and conflicting deadlines, contributes to a high level of job-related stress.

"A thorough knowledge of traffic is a primary skill needed for success. This includes the nitty-gritty of tariffs and anything else dealing with the traffic function. You also need an understanding of sales. It is good to understand marketing, forecasting, product development, and product capabilities. You have to be a decision maker. You must be innovative in presentations and skillful in communications. It's important that you are able to listen carefully. The ability to follow through and to be detail-oriented are also important skills.

"When I'm interviewing a job candidate, I consider the individual's ability to learn. I normally inquire as to grade point average and am interested in knowing if the person was independent in obtaining that education.

"I would suggest that students start at the very bottom; in this company, that means beginning as an order entry clerk and then becoming first a customer service representative and later a key account representative. It also means working in the warehouse and directly with the freight companies.

"There really is a need for sharp, capable, and creative young people. However, it is important for them to honestly evaluate their own needs and abilities, and associate these with their career objectives before they seek a position."

SELLING CAREERS[4]

What Is Personal Selling?

A bag of potato chips, a piece of construction equipment, a romance novel, a life insurance policy. These and thousands of

---

4 The material in this section is adapted by the authors from *Occupational Outlook Handbook*, 1992-93 Edition (Washington, D.C.: U.S. Department of Labor, May 1992), pp. 223-235.

other goods and services are bought and sold each day. Sales representatives are an important part of this process. They market products to manufacturers, wholesale and retail establishments, government agencies and other organizations, and final consumers. Whatever the type of good or service they sell, the primary job is to interact with their customers and provide the link between their firms and those customers.

Professional salespeople generate customer leads, ascertain needs, communicate with consumers, emphasize knowledge as well as persuasion, and provide service. Examples of professional sales personnel are stockbrokers, manufacturer sales representatives, real-estate brokers, and insurance agents--many of whom are college educated and engaged in long-term careers. Clerical sales personnel answer telephone inquiries, obtain stock from inventory, recommend the best brand in a product category, and complete transactions by receiving payments and packing products. Examples are retail, wholesale, and manufacturer sales clerks--many of whom are college students employed in part-time positions.

A strong emphasis on personal selling is often desirable. Large-volume customers want special attention and handling. Geographically concentrated consumers may be more effectively reached by salespeople than ads in mass media. Custom-made, expensive, and/or complex goods or services need detailed consumer information, demonstrations, and follow-up calls. Tangential sales services--such as training--may be requested. Some customer questions can be resolved only through personal selling. New products may require personal selling to gain channel-member acceptance. Finally, many organizational customers expect a high level of personal contact and service.

Personal selling provides individual attention for each consumer and passes along a lot of information. There is a two-way interaction between buyer and seller. Sales approaches can be adapted to the needs of specific consumers. Personal selling clinches sales and is usually the last stage in the consumer's decision process, taking place after an information search and exposure to ads. It holds on to repeat customers and those already convinced by advertising, resolves doubts or concerns of undecided consumers, and answers any remaining questions about price, warranty, and other factors.

At a number of companies, experience in sales is a prerequisite for future advancement in marketing management. Those companies believe that an individual person can really understand a business only if he or she has interacted with customers.

What Background Do You Need for a Sales Career?

The background needed for sales jobs varies by product line and market. A college degree is increasingly desirable for a job as a professional sales representative, particularly for career tracks in sales management. Nonetheless, some employers hire individuals with previous experience who do not yet have a college degree.

Many companies have formal training programs for beginning sales representatives that last up to two years. In some programs, trainees rotate among jobs in plants and offices to learn all phases of production, installation, and distribution of the product. In others, trainees take formal classroom instruction at the plant, followed by on-the-job training under the supervision of a field sales manager. At some firms, new workers are trained by accompanying more experienced salespeople on their calls. As these workers gain better familiarity with the companies' products and clients, they are given increasing responsibility until they are assigned their own territories.

Sales personnel must stay abreast of new products and the changing needs of customers. They may attend trade shows where innovations are displayed or conferences and conventions where they meet with other salespeople and clients to discuss new product developments. In addition, many firms sponsor meetings of their entire sales force where presentations are made on sales performance, product development, and profitability.

Sales representatives should be goal oriented, persuasive, and able to work independently. A pleasant personality and appearance, the ability to get along with people, and problem-solving skills also are important. Patience and perseverance are needed because completing a sale can take several months. Often, sales personnel should enjoy traveling because much of their time is spent visiting with current and prospective clients.

Salespeople analyze sales data and handle administrative duties, such as filing their expense account reports, scheduling appointments, and making travel plans. They also study literature about new and existing products, and monitor the sales, prices, and products of their competitors.

Frequently, a promotion takes the form of an assignment to a larger account or territory where commissions are likely to be greater. Experienced sales representatives may move into jobs as sales trainers--workers who train new employees on selling techniques and company policies and procedures. Those who have good sales records and leadership ability may advance to sales supervisor or district manager.

Jobs in Selling

Career opportunities in personal selling vary dramatically. In the United States alone, about 14 million people work in sales positions. Following are brief descriptions of just a few of the sales positions that are suitable for college graduates.

Industrial Sales Representatives

Manufacturers' and wholesalers' sales personnel spend a lot of their time traveling to and visiting with prospective buyers. During sales calls, they discuss customers' needs and suggest how their goods or services can meet those needs. They may show samples or catalogs describing their companies' products and inform customers about prices, availability, and how their products can save money and improve productivity. In addition, because of the vast number of manufacturers and wholesalers selling similar products, they try to stress the unique qualities of the goods and services offered by their particular firms. They also take orders and resolve any problems or complaints with the products.

Obtaining new accounts is an important part of this type of selling job. Salespeople follow leads suggested by current clients, as well as those derived from advertisements in trade journals and participation in trade shows and conferences. At times, they make "cold calls" upon potential clients. They may also have to meet with and entertain prospective clients during evenings and weekends.

Some salespeople have specialized duties. For example, sales engineers (who are among the most trained sales workers) typically are involved with products whose installation and optimal use require substantial expertise and support--items like main-frame computers, material-handling equipment, and numerical-control machinery. Besides providing information on their firms' products, they may recommend improved materials and machinery for a customer's manufacturing process, draw up plans of proposed machinery layouts, and estimate cost savings from the use of their equipment. They then present this information and negotiate the sale, a process that may take several months. They often work with engineers in their own companies, adapting products to customers' special needs.

Increasingly, sales representatives who do not have technical expertise work as a team with a technical specialist. For example, a sales representative could make the preliminary contact with customers, introduce company products, and close transactions. The technically trained person would attend the sales presentation to help with technical questions and concerns. In this way, the sales representative is able to spend more time maintaining and soliciting accounts and less time acquiring technical knowledge. After the sale, sales representatives may make frequent follow-up visits to ensure that the equipment is functioning properly; and they may even train their customers' employees as to how to operate and maintain the equipment.

Those selling consumer products often suggest to their dealer-customers how and where items should be displayed. In working with retailers, they may help arrange promotional programs and advertising.

Securities Sales Representatives

Most investors--whether individuals with a few hundred dollars to invest or large institutions with millions--use securities sales representatives when buying or selling stocks, bonds, shares in mutual funds, insurance annuities, certificates of deposit, or other financial products. Securities sales representatives often are known as account executives, registered representatives, or brokers.

When an investor wishes to buy or sell securities, sales representatives may relay the order through their companies' offices to the floor of the securities exchange, such as the New York Stock Exchange. There, specialized securities sales representatives (brokers' floor representatives) buy and sell the securities. If a security is not traded on an exchange, the sales representative sends the order to the firm's trading department which trades it directly with a dealer in the over-the-counter market. After a transaction is completed, a sales representative notifies the customer of the final price.

Securities sales representatives also provide many related services for customers. Depending on a customer's knowledge of the market, they may explain the meaning of stock market terms and trading practices; offer financial advice; devise an individual financial portfolio (which may include securities, life insurance, corporate and municipal bonds, mutual funds, certificates of deposit, annuities, and other investments); and offer suggestions on the purchase or sale of particular securities. Securities salespeople furnish information about the advantages and disadvantages of an investment based on each client's objective. They also supply the latest price quotations on any security in which the investor is interested, as well as data on the activities and financial positions of the companies issuing these securities.

Most securities sales representatives serve individual investors while some specialize in institutional investors. With institutional investing, sales representatives usually concentrate on one type of financial product such as stocks, bonds, options, annuities, or commodity futures. Some handle the sale of new issues, such as corporate securities issued to finance plant expansion.

The most important part of a sales representative's job is finding clients and building a customer base. Thus, beginning securities sales representatives spend much of their time in searching for customers--relying heavily on telephone solicitation. They may meet some clients through business and social contacts. Many sales representatives find it useful to get additional exposure by teaching adult education investment courses or by giving lectures at libraries or social clubs.

The overwhelming majority of entrants to this occupation are college graduates. Even though employers seldom require specialized academic training, courses in business administration, economics, and finance are helpful.

Securities sales representatives must meet state licensing requirements, which generally include passing an examination and, in some cases, furnishing a personal bond. Furthermore, salespeople must register as representatives of their firms according to the regulations of the securities exchanges where they do business or the National Association of Securities Dealers, Inc. (NASD). Before beginners can qualify as registered representatives, they must pass the General Securities Registered Representative Examination, administered by the NASD. Most states require a second examination--the Uniform Securities Agents State Law Examination. These tests measure the prospective representative's knowledge of the securities business, customer protection requirements, and record-keeping procedures.

Many employers provide on-the-job training to help their sales representatives meet the requirements for registration. In most firms, the training period generally takes about four months. Trainees in large firms may receive classroom instruction in securities analysis, effective speaking, and the finer points of selling; take courses offered by business schools or other institutions and associations; and undergo a period of on-the-job training lasting up to two years. In small firms, sales representatives generally receive training in outside institutions and on the job. Many trainees take correspondence courses in preparation for the securities examinations.

The principal form of advancement for securities sales representatives is an increase in the number and size of the accounts they handle. Although beginners usually service the accounts of individual investors, eventually they may handle very large institutional accounts such as those of banks and pension funds. Some experienced representatives become branch office managers and supervise other sales personnel while also continuing to provide services for their own customers. A few representatives advance to top management positions or become partners in firms.

Services Sales Representatives

Services sales representatives are involved with a wide variety of services, from pest control and printing services to advertising services and telecommunications systems. Sales personnel for data-processing services firms sell complex services like sales-analysis, payroll-processing, inventory-control, and financial-reporting systems. Educational services sales representatives might persuade states to use a particular licensing examination on insurance laws and regulations. Hotel sales personnel contact government, business, and social groups in order to solicit convention and conference business; and they contact prospective clients, determine their needs, outline the types and prices of the services offered by their hotels, and prepare contracts when clients reserve space at the hotels.

Fund-raising personnel plan programs to raise money for charities or other causes, such as the Special Olympics for handicapped children and mentally retarded adults. They write, telephone, or visit potential contributors and persuade them to donate money by explaining the purpose and benefits of various sports programs. They also may organize volunteers and plan special events to raise money.

Sales representatives for temporary-help services firms locate and acquire clients who will hire the firms' employees. Telephone-services sales personnel contact and visit commercial customers to review their telephone systems, analyze communications needs, and recommend services such as installation of additional telephone instruments, lines, and switchboard systems. Other representatives sell automotive leasing, public utility, burial, shipping, protective, and management consulting services.

Despite the diversity of services being sold, the jobs of virtually all services sales representatives have much in common. First, all sales representatives must fully understand and be able to discuss the services their firms offer. Second, the procedures they follow are similar. They develop lists of prospective clients through selected use of telephone and business directories--asking business associates and customers for leads, and looking for new clients as they cover their assigned territories. Sometimes, they acquire clients through persons who call to inquire about the firms' services. Then, they meet with clients and explain how the services offered can meet their needs, sometimes by using literature or demonstrations to show the firms' services. They answer questions about the nature and cost of the services and try to persuade potential customers to purchase the services. If they fail to make a sale on the first visit, they may follow-up with more visits, letters, and phone calls. After making a sale, representatives call on their customers to see that the services have met their needs, to determine if additional services are needed, and to obtain referrals.

Because services sales representatives obtain many new accounts through referrals, it is important that they maintain regular contact with their clients to ensure their satisfaction with the services. Developing satisfied clients who will continue to use the services and will recommend them to other potential customers is an important key to success. Like other types of sales jobs, a services sales representative's reputation is very important to his or her success.

Some aspects of service sales work vary with the kind of service sold. Selling highly technical services, such as communications systems or computer consulting services, usually involves more complex and lengthy sales processes. In these situations, salespeople usually operate according to policies outlined in their firms' marketing and business plans. Such work plans identity prospective clients, establish marketing strategies, and set forth staff responsibilities and time-tables to achieve goals. In selling technical services, sales representatives must become familiar with the intricacies of customers' operations so as to best serve their needs. Sales representatives often work as part of a team and receive technical assistance from support personnel. For example, those who sell data processing services might work with a systems engineer, and those who sell telephone services might receive technical assistance from a communications consultant. Because of the time between the initial contact with a customer and the actual sale, representatives who sell technical services generally work with several customers at one time. Since prospective sales might be at different stages of the process, representatives must be well organized and efficient in scheduling their time. On the other hand, some representatives deal exclusively with one large client. Selling less complex services, like linen supply, detective, or exterminating services, generally involves simpler and shorter sales processes.

Many employers require that services sales representatives have college degrees, but specific requirements vary depending on the services that a particular firm sells. Companies that market educational services prefer individuals with advanced degrees in marketing or related fields. Hotels frequently seek graduates from college hotel administration programs, and companies selling computer services and telephone systems prefer sales personnel who have backgrounds in computer science or engineering. Courses in business, economics, and marketing can be helpful in obtaining most jobs as services sales representatives.

Some firms conduct formal intensive training programs for sales representatives. Individuals learn about the companies' operations and services. They receive instruction in various sales techniques, such as prospecting for clients, probing customer needs, interviewing, sales presentations, and closing sales. They may receive motivational and sensitivity training to help them understand different personality types and make them more effective in dealing with people. Sales representatives may also attend seminars on a wide range of subjects given by outside training institutions, such as technical schools and colleges. In addition, frequent "in-house" training sessions acquaint them with new services and help them maintain and update sales techniques.

Sales representatives who have good sales records and leadership abilities may advance to sales supervisors, then branch or district managers. Frequent contact with business-people in other firms can provide sales workers with leads about outside job openings, thus facilitating advancement possibilities. Some go into business for themselves or find opportunities in services advertising or marketing research.

WHOLESALING AND RETAILING CAREERS[5]

What Are Wholesaling and Retailing?

Wholesaling involves the buying or handling of merchandise and the subsequent resale of that merchandise, along with related customer services, to organizational users, retailers, and/or other wholesalers--but not the sale of significant volume to final consumers. With manufacturer wholesaling, a manufacturer undertakes all the wholesaling functions itself. With merchant wholesaling, firms not affiliated with manufacturers buy, take title, and take possession of products for further resale. In agent and broker wholesaling, firms not affiliated with manufacturers provide wholesale functions; but, they do not take title to goods.

Retailing encompasses those business activities involved with the sale of goods and services to the final consumer for personal, family, or household use. Among the more popular retail formats are convenience stores, supermarkets, specialty stores, department stores, and retail catalog showrooms. In recent years, retail franchising has grown substantially. With retail franchising, there is a contractual arrangement between a franchisor (such as McDonald's) and a retail franchisee (the owner-operator) which allows the franchisee to conduct a given form of business under an established name and according to a specific set of rules.

Because of the interest in buying and merchandising careers, this job category is the focus for the following discussion. However, please keep in mind that there are numerous other opportunities in wholesaling and retailing--in areas like operations, marketing research, advertising, and inventory management. Virtually all of the job titles that were cited in Table 1, as well as those discussed earlier in this chapter, are available in the wholesaling and retailing industries. These opportunities include millions and millions of full- and part-time jobs in both the wholesaling and retailing sectors.

Wholesale and Retail Buyers and Merchandise Managers

Shop until you drop! Just like final consumers, wholesale and retail buyers and merchandise managers do just that. Working for wholesalers and retailers, these buyers purchase products for resale. Merchandise managers supervise the buyers and set

---

5 The material in this section is adapted by the authors from *Occupational Outlook Handbook*, 1992-93 Edition (Washington, D.C.: U.S. Department of Labor, May 1992), pp. 62-63.

general buying and pricing policy for their departments, divisions, or stores. Regardless of what they buy--from clothing to machinery---they seek the best available products at the lowest possible prices. Working with sales and marketing managers, they also determine how merchandise will be distributed and marketed.

Wholesale and retail buyers are a key part of a complex system of production, distribution, and merchandising that caters to the vast variety of consumer needs and desires. Buyers employed by large and medium-sized firms usually specialize in acquiring one or two lines of products. Buyers who work for small stores may purchase the firms' entire stock of products. Wholesale buyers purchase directly from manufacturers or from other wholesalers for resale to retail firms or to commercial establishments and other institutions. Retail buyers purchase from wholesale firms or directly from manufacturers for resale to the public.

The success of any wholesale or retail firm depends on its ability to sell merchandise. Because buyers determine which products their establishments will sell, it is essential that they be knowledgeable about the products they are buying and know what will appeal to consumers. These skills usually are developed through several years of experience as an assistant buyer--an entry-level position. Assistant buyers have many of the same duties as buyers, but they also have the guidance of the experienced buyers to help them.

In order to purchase the best selection of goods, buyers must be familiar with the merchandise, domestic and foreign manufacturers and distributors, and sales records. Thus, they must keep informed about changes in existing products and the development of new ones. To learn about merchandise, buyers read industry periodicals, attend trade shows and conferences, and visit manufacturers' showrooms.

Both wholesalers and retailers are continuing to expand their use of computers, which has simplified many routine buying functions and improved efficiency. Traditionally, buyers have relied on sales staff and inventory counts to determine which products were selling. Now, computerized systems have dramatically changed this. For example, cash registers connected to computers, known as point-of-sale terminals, allow organizations to maintain centralized, up-to-date sales and inventory records. Information such as the price, color, or model number is often fed into the computer using bar codes or magnetic strips attached to the goods. This information can then be used to produce weekly sales reports that reflect the types of products in demand. With the data generated by these systems, buyers spend their time analyzing data and not collecting them.

In addition to monitoring company sales, buyers use their computers to gain instant access to the specifications for thousands of commodities, inventory records, and their customers' purchase records. Buyers also follow ads in newspapers and other media to check their competitors' sales activities and watch general economic conditions to anticipate consumer buying patterns.

Once buyers decide what to purchase, they determine from whom to purchase. They base their decisions on price, availability, reliability of the suppliers, and selection. Buyers' responsibilities have expanded with the use of private-label merchandise, which is produced for a particular wholesaler or retailer and carries the name designated by that firm. In any case, buyers often work closely with vendors to obtain the desired products. Because most buyers have a limited budget, they must plan their purchases to keep needed items in stock, but also allow for unexpected purchases when a "good buy" presents itself.

The ordering process varies by company. Many orders are placed during buying trips, but they are also made when wholesalers' and manufacturers' sales personnel call on buyers to display their merchandise. Some companies are linked with manufacturers or wholesalers by electronic purchasing systems, which speed selection and ordering and provide information on availability and shipment. Often, assistant buyers are responsible for placing orders and checking shipments.

Many buyers and merchandise managers assist in the planning and implementation of sales promotion programs. Working with merchandising executives, they determine the nature of the sale and buy accordingly. They also work with advertising personnel to create ad campaigns. For example, they may determine the media in which the advertisement will be placed-- newspaper, direct mail, television, or some combination of these. In addition, retail buyers often visit the selling floor to ensure that the goods are being displayed properly.

Buying is not an entry-level job. Qualified persons typically begin as assistant buyers or trainees. Firms prefer to hire applicants who are familiar with the merchandise they sell, as well as with wholesaling and retailing practices. Some firms promote qualified employees to assistant buyer positions; some recruit and train college graduates as assistant buyers. Most employers use a combination of methods.

Educational requirements for entry-level assistant buying positions tend to vary with the size of the organization. The largest stores and distributors seek applicants who have already completed associate or bachelor's degree programs from any field of study. Training and job experience introduce the new worker to retail or wholesale trade operations and the policies fundamental to merchandising and management.

Although training periods vary in length, they can last for several years. Most trainees begin by selling merchandise, supervising sales workers, checking invoices on merchandise received, and keeping track of stock on hand--although the widespread use of computers in both wholesale and retail trade has simplified some of these tasks. As they progress, trainees are given more buying-related responsibilities.

To maintain their effectiveness, buyers must constantly be aware of what their customers want. They take courses in merchandising techniques, attend trade shows and conferences, and read industry publications to stay abreast of new developments and products.

Persons who wish to become buyers should be good at planning and decision making and be interested in merchandising. Anticipating consumer preferences and ensuring that goods are in stock when they are needed require resourcefulness, good judgment, and self-confidence. Buyers must be able to make quick decisions and take risks. Marketing skills and the ability to identify products that will sell are also important. Employers often look for leadership abilities and communications skills because buyers spend a large portion of their time supervising assistant buyers and dealing with manufacturers' sales personnel and store executives. In addition, buyers need physical stamina to keep up with the fast-paced nature of their work.

Experienced buyers may advance by moving to departments that manages a larger volume or by becoming merchandise managers. Others "jump to the other side of the fence" and go to work in sales for manufacturers.

Employment of buyers and merchandise managers is expected to increase about as fast as the average for all occupations through the year 2005. However, over the past few years, the organizational structure of wholesaling and retailing has been changing. Many companies have acquired or merged with others. When buying functions are centralized by the new organization, fewer buyers and managers are needed.

Buying and merchandising positions attract many college graduates; therefore, the number of qualified job seekers may exceed the number of openings. Prospects are likely to be best for those with previous wholesale or retail trade experience.

CHAPTER THREE

MARKETING-RELATED JOBS AND INTERNSHIPS DURING COLLEGE

OVERVIEW

In planning for your career, a well-balanced approach during college is often the key to long-run success. But what does this mean? A person should take his or her college education seriously, participate in co-curricular and extra-curricular activities, and begin to acquire meaningful work experience.

With regard to work experience, it is becoming more and more important to potential employers that you can demonstrate the following:

. Prior exposure to the workplace (to show that you understand what it is like to work and that you are a responsible individual)
. Evidence that you have a sustained commitment to working (which indicates whether you have worked over a period of years rather than just during your senior year)
. General business skills (such as how to operate a cash register or proofread ad copy)
. Specialized business skills (such as how to interview the respondents in a marketing research survey or how to calculate the retail markup for an item)
. Supervisory skills (to show that you have been promoted and that you have been learning how to manage others)

While in college, you will have many choices about working. Here are some of them:

Should I work at all? Yes. If you concentrate all of your efforts on classes and school-related activities, you will not be giving yourself the opportunity to gain "real world" experience. In today's competitive job market, this will almost certainly place you at a significant disadvantage with regard to your classmates.

Should I settle for any kind of job that is available? If no "good" jobs are available, you should undertake the best available one (even being an usher at a movie theater or a counterperson at a fast-food restaurant). By doing so, you will gain exposure to the workplace and demonstrate that you have a sustained commitment to working. Employers will be impressed by your willingness to take on unglamorous tasks. In addition, you will be learning basic business skills.

Nonetheless, as you move through college, your jobs should become more career-related. In your freshman and sophomore years at school, it is quite all right to work at any job. In your junior and senior years, you should seek positions that are more related to your future career. Be open-minded and creative in this regard. For example, selling ad space for your school newspaper or managing a nearby stationery store are career-related jobs for a person interested in advertising or retailing.

<u>Should I work only in my chosen area of interest?</u> As a rule, no. First, if you decide only to work in your area of interest, you may sit out a good portion of your college years without any job. Second, employers usually want to see that you have gained a number of general skills (such as how to interact with people, how to be a team player, what it is like to show up for work every day, and so on) and that you are realistic and flexible regarding the tasks you will perform when you obtain an entry-level, full-time position after college.

<u>Should I work for a small firm or a large one?</u> In a small firm, you are more likely to work closely with the owner of that firm and perform a wide variety of tasks. Your job may vary greatly from day to day, and there will probably be little emphasis on formal training. In a large firm, you are more likely to work closely with the manager of a given department and perform a narrower variety of tasks. Your job will likely vary rather little from day to day, and there will be some emphasis on formal training (depending on the job). Either type of firm has the potential to fulfill your needs. Again, be open minded and carefully look at the attributes of alternative jobs (not just at alternative employers).

<u>Should I work for free to gain experience?</u> This is a question that only you can answer, based on your financial needs, your long-term goals, and your personal perceptions about nonpaid work. But keep these points in mind. Working for free for a nonprofit organization may be rewarding in both experiential and societal terms. Working for free for a profit-oriented firm may provide good experience in your chosen field, and this may be the only way that you can gain the background you desire. In addition, after graduation from college, you may have an advantage in seeking a full-time position with a firm where you have already worked. Advertising agencies and media companies typically offer only nonpaid positions for college students.

<u>Should I work in a formal internship program?</u> Again, this depends on your personal goals. With a formal internship program, you will typically receive college credit and interact with both a faculty advisor and an advisor at the participating company. You will be able to work only for an approved company in an approved job. A minimum number of work hours per week will be specified. At some colleges, interns work about 12 hours per week over the course of a semester or full time over a summer. At other colleges, "co-op" programs enable students to spread their education over more years while they spend more time out in the workplace. In either case, the on-the-job emphasis will be on training, and academic assignments (such as a term paper summarizing the concepts learned during the internship) will be required. Through an internship, the

best of your college and work experiences will be combined. After college graduation, successful interns often accept permanent positions with the sponsoring companies.

Sometimes, students get too hung up on the word "internship." An internship is a valuable tool for those who want a formal program, who desire academic credit, and who want to be closely supervised. On the other hand, traditional jobs may be more flexible in their requirements, do not require academic assignments, and will be more controllable by you.

FIRMS WITH MARKETING-RELATED JOBS AND INTERNSHIPS FOR COLLEGE STUDENTS

Please note: The firms listed below regularly employ college students in marketing-related jobs and internships. In any given year, a particular company may decide to hire a number of people for marketing-related positions or may not have any openings. Contact the individual firms in which you have a job or internship interest for further information.

The mailing address, telephone number, and principal business for each of the firms cited in this section may be found in Chapter Four of this career guide:

ABRAHAM & STRAUS
ADDISON-WESLEY PUBLISHING COMPANY
ADP
AETNA LIFE & CASUALTY COMPANY, INC.
AGWAY, INC.
AIR PRODUCTS & CHEMICALS, INC.
ALLSTATE INSURANCE COMPANY
AMERICAN INTERNATIONAL GROUP
AT&T
BACKER SPIELVOGEL BATES WORLDWIDE
BAXTER HEALTHCARE CORPORATION
BBDO WORLDWIDE, INC.
BOZELL, INC.
BURKE MARKETING RESEARCH
BURLINGTON INDUSTRIES, INC.
CHRYSLER CORPORATION
CIGNA CORPORATION
LIZ CLAIBORNE, INC.
COCA-COLA USA
CODEX CORPORATION
DDB NEEDHAM WORLDWIDE, INC.
R. R. DONNELLY & SONS COMPANY
DOW CHEMICAL, USA
DOW CORNING CORPORATION
E. I. DU PONT DE NEMOURS AND COMPANY
EASTMAN KODAK COMPANY

EATON CORPORATION
EDISON BROTHERS STORES, INC.
ELECTRONIC DATA SYSTEMS CORPORATION
EXXON CORPORATION
FIELDCREST CANNON, INC.
FOOTE, CONE & BELDING COMMUNICATIONS
GENERAL MOTORS CORPORATION
GTE CORPORATION
HAGGAR APPAREL COMPANY
HALLMARK CARDS, INC.
IBM CORPORATION
ITT SHERATON CORPORATION
KELLOGG COMPANY
LAZARUS DEPARTMENT STORES
ELI LILLY AND COMPANY
R. H. MACY & COMPANY, INC.
TJ MAXX
THOM McCAN SHOE COMPANY
McCANN-ERICKSON WORLDWIDE
McDONALD'S RESTAURANT CORPORATION
MCI TELECOMMUNICATIONS
MEAD CORPORATION
MERCK & COMPANY, INC.
METROPOLITAN LIFE AND AFFILIATED COMPANIES
MICROSOFT CORPORATION
NCR CORPORATION
NEW YORK LIFE INSURANCE COMPANY
OGILVY & MATHER WORLDWIDE, INC.
OWENS-CORNING FIBERGLAS CORPORATION
J. C. PENNEY COMPANY, INC.
PRUDENTIAL INSURANCE COMPANY OF AMERICA
SAKS FIFTH AVENUE
SKY CHEFS
SOUTHWESTERN BELL CORPORATION
STEELCASE, INC.
TANDY CORPORATION (RADIO SHACK)
J. WALTER THOMPSON COMPANY
WAL-MART STORES, INC.
WARNER-LAMBERT COMPANY
WHIRLPOOL CORPORATION
XEROX CORPORATION
YOUNG & RUBICAM, INC.

CHAPTER FOUR

A LISTING OF 500 FIRMS REGULARLY SEEKING COLLEGE GRADUATES FOR MARKETING-RELATED CAREERS

Please note: The firms listed below regularly seek out college graduates for marketing-related careers. In any given year, a particular company may decide to hire a number of people for marketing-related positions or not have any openings. Contact the individual firms in which you have a career interest for further information.

ABBOTT LABORATORIES
Corporate Placement
Abbott Park, IL 60064
  Principal Business: Manufacturing and marketing of health-care products
  Contact: Manager of College Relations
  Telephone: (708) 937-7000

ABITIBI-PRICE CORPORATION
3250 West Big Beaver Road
Troy, MI 48084
  Principal Business: Manufacturing and marketing of building products
  Contact: Director of Human Resources
  Telephone: (313) 649-3300

ABRAHAM & STRAUS
420 Fulton Street
Brooklyn, NY 11201
  Principal Business: Department store retailing
  Contact: Recruitment Director
  Telephone: (718) 802-7500

ACE HARDWARE CORPORATION
2200 Kensington Court
Oak Brook, IL 60521
  Principal Business: Hardware-store wholesaling cooperative
  Contact: Personnel Administration Representative

ADDISON-WESLEY PUBLISHING COMPANY
Jacob Way
Reading, MA 01867
  Principal Business: Publishing and marketing of textbooks
  Contact: Senior Human Resources Representative
  Telephone: (617) 944-3700

ADP
Employer Services Group
One ADP Boulevard
Roseland, NJ 07068
  Principal Business: Computerized business (employer) services

Contact: College Relations
Telephone: (201) 994-5516

ADVANCED TELEMARKETING CORPORATION
8001 Bent Branch
Irving, TX 75063
  Principal Business: Direct-marketing services
  Contact: Recruitment
  Telephone: (214) 830-1829

AETNA LIFE & CASUALTY COMPANY, INC.
151 Farmington Avenue
Hartford, CT 06156
  Principal Business: Insurance and other financial services
  Contact: College Relations
  Telephone: (203) 273-4129

AGWAY, INC.
333 Butternut Drive
Syracuse, NY 13221
  Principal Business: Manufacturing and marketing of food and other products
  Contact: Manager of Recruitment and Management Development
  Telephone: (315) 449-6591

AIR PRODUCTS & CHEMICALS, INC.
7201 Hamilton Boulevard
Allentown, PA 18195
  Principal Business: Marketing of industrial gases, chemicals, equipment, and technology
  Contact: University Relations
  Telephone: (215) 481-4918

ALBERTO-CULVER COMPANY
2525 Armitage Avenue
Melrose Park, IL 60160
  Principal Business: Manufacturing and marketing of personal-care, household, and grocery products
  Contact: Corporate Employment Manager

ALLEN-BRADLEY
1201 South Second Street
Milwaukee, Wl 53204

Principal Business: Manufacturing
and marketing of industrial
automation controls, electronics
products, and communication
systems
Contact: College Recruitment
Telephone: (414) 382-2978

ALLIED-SIGNAL, INC.
Columbia Road & Park Avenue
P.O. Box 1021R
Morristown, NJ 07962
Principal Business: Manufacturing and
marketing of chemicals, fibers, and
other products
Contact: Manager of Human
Resources
Telephone: (708) 391-2293

ALLSTATE INSURANCE COMPANY
Allstate Plaza South
Northbrook, IL 60062
Principal Business: Insurance and
other financial services
Contact: Employment Manager
Telephone: (708) 402-7140

ALUMINUM COMPANY OF AMERICA (ALCOA)
1501 Alcoa Building
Pittsburgh, PA 15219
Principal Business: Manufacturing and
marketing of aluminum products
Contact: Professional Employment
Telephone: (412) 553-2337

AMERADA HESS CORPORATION
1185 Avenue of the Americas
New York, NY 10036
Principal Business: Petroleum
refining and marketing
Contact: Manager of Corporate
Recruiting & College Relations
Telephone: (21) 536-8175

AMERICAN AIRLINES, INC.
P.O. Box 619616, MD 5105
Dallas/Fort Worth Airport
Dallas, TX 75261
Principal Business: Air
transportation
Contact: College Relations
Telephone: (817) 967-1435

AMERICAN BRANDS
1700 East Putnam Avenue
P.O. Box 819
Old Greenwich, CT 06870

Principal Business: Diversified
manufacturing and services
Contact: Personnel Department
Telephone: (203) 698-5000

AMERICAN DRUG STORES
1818 Swift Drive
Oak Brook, IL 60521
Principal Business: Drugstore
retailing
Contact: Director of Recruiting &
College Relations
Telephone: (708) 572-5294

AMERICAN EXPRESS COMPANY
American Express Tower
World Financial Center
New York, NY 10285
Principal Business: Financial
services
Contact: Personnel Department
Telephone: (212) 640-2000

AMERICAN FROZEN FOODS, INC.
355 Benton Street
Stratford, CT 06497
Principal Business: Shop-at-home food
delivery services
Contact: Director of Recruitment
Telephone: (800) 233-5554, Extension
3385

AMERICAN GENERAL CORPORATION
2929 Allen Parkway
Houston, TX 77253
Principal Business: Financial
services
Contact: Manager of Employment
Telephone: (713) 831-1160

AMERICAN GENERAL FINANCE
601 Northwest Second Street
Evansville, IN 47708
Principal Business: Financial
services
Contact: Manager of Employment
Telephone: (812) 468-5525

AMERICAN HOME PRODUCTS CORPORATION
685 Third Avenue
New York, NY 10017
Principal Business: Manufacturing and
marketing of personal-care and food
products
Contact: Personnel Department
Telephone: (212) 878-5000

AMERICAN INTERNATIONAL GROUP

70 Pine Street
New York, NY 10270
  Principal Business: Insurance and
  other financial services
  Contact: Manager of College
  Relations
  Telephone: (212) 770-3564
AMERICAN NATIONAL CAN COMPANY
8770 Bryn Mawr
Chicago, IL 60631
  Principal Business: Manufacturing and
  marketing of packaging products
  Contact: Manager of Personnel
  Telephone: (312) 399-3208
AMERICAN STANDARDS TESTING BUREAU, INC.
40 Water Street
New York, NY 10004
  Principal Business: Scientific,
  technical, and management consulting
  services
  Contact: Director of Professional
  Staffing
  Telephone: (212) 943-3160
AMERISURE COMPANIES
28 West Adams
Detroit, MI 48226
  Principal Business: Insurance
  services
  Contact: Human Resources
  Department
  Telephone: (313) 965-8600
AMERITECH SERVICES
2000 West Ameritech Center Drive
Hoffman Estates, IL 60196
  Principal Business: Telecommuni-
  cations services and equipment
  Contact: Manager of Regional Human
  Resources
  Telephone: (708) 248-3291
AMES DEPARTMENT STORES, INC.
2418 Main Street
Rocky Hill, CT 06067
  Principal Business: Discount
  department-store retailing
  Contact: Manager of Field Planning
  and Placement
  Telephone: (203) 257-2156
AMOCO CORPORATION
200 E. Randolph Drive
Chicago, IL 60601
  Principal Business: Petroleum

refining and marketing
  Contact: Director of Corporate
  Relations
  Telephone: (312) 856-3870
AMP INCORPORATED
470 Friendship Road
Harrisburg, PA 17105
  Principal Business: Manufacturing and
  marketing of electrical devices
  Contact: College Relations Manager
  Telephone: (717) 780-6680
AMPEX CORPORATION
401 Broadway
Redwood City, CA 94063
  Principal Business: Manufacturing and
  marketing of video and other tape
  products
  Contact: Manager of Human Resources
  Telephone: (415) 367-2626
AMWAY CORPORATION
7575 Fulton Street East
Ada, MI 49355
  Principal Business: Direct selling and
  manufacturing of consumer products
  Contact: College Relations
  Telephone: (616) 676-6000
ANDERSONS MANAGEMENT CORPORATION
1200 Dussel Drive
P.O. Box 119
Maumee, OH 43537
  Principal Business: Manufacturing and
  marketing of lawn fertilizer and
  agricultural products, specialty
  retailing
  Contact: Recruitment Manager
ANHEUSER BUSCH COMPANIES, INC.
One Busch Place
St. Louis, MO 63118
  Principal Business: Manufacturing and
  marketing of beer and food products
  Contact: Supervisor of College Relations
  Telephone: (314) 577-2470
APPLE COMPUTER, INC.
20525 Mariani Avenue
Cupertino, CA 95014
  Principal Business: Manufacturing and
  marketing of computers and software
  Contact: College Relations Manager
  Telephone: (408) 974-3010
ARATEX SERVICES, INC.
115 North First Street

CHAPTER FOUR: FIRMS WITH MARKETING-RELATED POSITIONS

Burbank, CA 91502
  Principal Business: Textile and
  uniform rental services
  Contact: Director of Compensation/EEO
  Telephone: (818) 973-3500
ARCHER DANIELS MIDLAND COMPANY
466 Faries Parkway
Decatur, IL 62525
  Principal Business: Processing and
  marketing of agricultural products
  Contact: College Recruiting
  Coordinator
  Telephone: (217) 424-5653
ARCO CHEMICAL COMPANY
3801 West Chester Pike
Newtown Square, PA 19073
  Principal Business: Manufacturing and
  marketing of chemical and specialty
  products
  Contact: College Relations Manager
  Telephone: (215) 359-7024
ARCO PRODUCTS COMPANY
1055 West Seventh Street
Los Angeles, CA 90051
  Principal Business: Petroleum
  refining and marketing
  Contact: Human Resources
  Representative
  Telephone: (213) 486-3248
ARKANSAS BEST CORPORATION
P.O. Box 305
Fort Smith, AR 72902
  Principal Business: Transportation
  and information services
  Contact: Senior Manager of Services
  and Human Resources
  Telephone: (501) 784-8491
ARKWRIGHT MUTUAL INSURANCE COMPANY
225 Wyman Street
Waltham, MA 02254
  Principal Business: Insurance and
  other financial services
  Contact: Personnel Manager
  Telephone: (617) 890-9300, Extension
  3710
ARMCO INC.
703 Curtis Street
Middletown, OH 45043
  Principal Business: Manufacturing and
  marketing of metal materials
  Contact: Manager of Human Resources &

Staff Services
  Telephone: (513) 425-2939
ARMSTRONG WORLD INDUSTRIES, INC.
P.O. Box 3001
Lancaster, PA 17604
  Principal Business: Manufacturing and
  marketing of interior furnishings and
  other products
  Contact: Manager of College Relations
  Telephone: (717) 396-2541
ARMY & AIR FORCE EXCHANGE SERVICE (AAFES)
P.O. Box 660202
PE-C3
Dallas, TX 75266
  Principal Business: General merchandise
  and food retailing
  Contact: Chief of Recruitment & Execu-
  tive Development
  Telephone: (214) 312-2276
ASHLAND CHEMICAL, INC.
P.O. Box 2219
Columbus, OH 43216
  Principal Business: Manufacturing and
  marketing of chemical products
  Contact: College Relations Administrator
  Telephone: (614) 889-4053
ASHLAND OIL, INC.
P.O. Box 391
Ashland, KY 41114
  Principal Business: Diversified energy
  manufacturing and marketing
  Contact: Employment Supervisor
  Telephone: (606) 329-4115
AT&T
100 Southgate Parkway
Morristown, NJ 07960
  Principal Business: Telecommunications
  services and equipment
  Contact: College Recruiting Manager
  Telephone: (201) 898-8394
AVANTEK, INC.
481 Cottonwood Drive
Milpitas, CA 95035
  Principal Business: Manufacturing and
  marketing of microwave components and
  subassemblies
  Contact: Manager of College Relations
  Telephone: (408) 970-2208
AVERY DENNISON
250 Chester St.
Painesville, OH 44077

50

Principal Business: Manufacturing
and marketing of pressure-sensitive
papers and industrial tapes
Contact: Manager of Human Resources
Telephone: (216) 357-4902

AVIS RENT A CAR SYSTEMS, INC.
1650 Old Bayshore Highway
Burlingame, CA 94010
Principal Business: Vehicle rental
services
Contact: Director of Human Resources
Telephone: (415) 259-1158

BABCOCK & WILCOX
P.O. Box 61038
New Orleans, LA 70161
Principal Business: Manufacturing and
marketing of steam generating and
associated equipment
Contact: Manager of College
Recruiting
Telephone: (504) 587-6400

BACKER SPIELVOGEL BATES WORLDWIDE
405 Lexington Avenue
New York, NY 10174
Principal Business: Advertising
services
Contact: Personnel Department
Telephone: (212) 297-7000

BAKERS/LEEDS SHOE STORES
P.O. Box 14020
St. Louis, MO 63102
Principal Business: Footwear
retailing
Contact: Vice-President of Store
Operations
Telephone: (800) 458-3304

BAKERS SQUARE RESTAURANTS
5275 Quincy Street
Mounds View, MN 55112
Principal Business: Specialty
retailing
Contact: Regional Recruiter
Telephone: (612) 784-3715 or (708)
747-8640

BALTIMORE GAS & ELECTRIC COMPANY
P.O. Box 1475
Baltimore, MD 21203
Principal Business: Electric & gas
utility services
Contact: Supervisor of Employment
Planning & Support

Telephone: (301) 234-6163

BANK OF AMERICA
One South Van Ness Avenue
San Francisco, CA 94137
Principal Business: Financial services
Contact: Manager of College Relations
Telephone: (415) 241-3065

BANKERS TRUST
280 Park Avenue
New York, NY 10017
Principal Business: Financial services
Contact: Manager of College & University
Relations
Telephone: (212) 454-1790

BAROID CORPORATION
3000 North Sam Houston Parkway, East
Houston, TX 77032
Principal Business: Petroleum services
Contact: Human Resources Representative
Telephone: (713) 987-5669

BASF CORPORATION
100 Cherry Hill Road
Parsippany, NJ 07054
Principal Business: Manufacturing and
marketing of industrial chemicals and
other products
Contact: Manager of Professional
Development Programs
Telephone: (201) 316-3262

BASKIN-ROBBINS, INC.
31 Baskin-Robbins Place
Glendale, CA 91201
Principal Business: Ice-cream
franchising
Contact: Personnel Department
Telephone: (818) 956-0031

BAXTER HEALTHCARE CORPORATION
One Baxter Parkway
Deerfield, IL 60015
Principal Business: Manufacturing and
marketing of health-care products
Contact: Director of College Relations
and Staffing
Telephone: (708) 948-2000

BBDO WORLDWIDE, INC.
1285 Avenue of the Americas
New York, NY 10016
Principal Business: Advertising
services
Contact: Personnel Department
Telephone: (212) 459-5000

BECTON DICKINSON AND COMPANY
One Becton Drive
Franklin Lakes, NJ 07471
Principal Business: Manufacturing
and marketing of health-care
products
Contact: Director of Human
Resources
Telephone: (201) 848-6827

BELDON DIVISION
Cooper Industries, Inc.
P.O. Box 1980
Richmond, IN 47375
Principal Business: Manufacturing and
marketing of electronic wire and
cable fiber optics
Contact: Personnel Manager

BELK STORES SERVICES, INC.
2801 Tyvola Road, West
Charlotte, NC 28217
Principal Business: Department store
retailing
Contact: Director of Human Resources
Planning
Telephone: (704) 357-1000

BELL ATLANTIC CORPORATION
One Parkway, Third Floor
Philadelphia, PA 19102
Principal Business: Telecommunica-
tions services and equipment
Contact: Manager of Management
Employment
Telephone: (215) 466-5205

BELLSOUTH CORPORATION
1155 Peachtree Street, Northeast
Atlanta, GA 30367
Principal Business: Telecommunica-
tions services and equipment
Contact: Manager of Management
Employment
Telephone: (404) 249-2175

BIG STAR FOODS
2251 North Sylvan Road
East Point, GA 30344
Principal Business: Supermarket
retailing
Contact: Associate Human Relations
Specialist
Telephone: (404) 765-8300

BLOCKBUSTER VIDEO
601 Gateway Boulevard

South San Francisco, CA 94080
Principal Business: Video
retailing
Contact: Area Recruiter
Telephone: (415) 873-6400

BLOOMINGDALE'S
1000 Third Avenue
New York, NY 10022
Principal Business: Department store
retailing
Contact: Manager of College Recruitment
Telephone: (212) 705-2383

BON MARCHE
Third & Pine
Seattle, WA 98181
Principal Business: Department store
retailing
Contact: Executive Placement Manager
Telephone: (206) 344-7292

ROBERT BOSCH CORPORATION, SALES GROUP
2800 South 25th Avenue
Broadview, IL 60153
Principal Business: Marketing of
automotive, mobile communications, and
household products
Contact: Senior Personnel Representative
Telephone: (708) 865-5485

THE BOSTON COMPANY
One Cabot Road
Medford, MA 02155
Principal Business: Financial services
Contact: Manager of Employment
Telephone: (617) 382-9182

BOZELL, INC.
40 West 23rd Street
New York, NY 10010
Principal Business: Advertising services
Contact: Personnel Department
Telephone: (212) 727-5000

BP AMERICA, INC.
200 Public Square
Cleveland, OH 44114
Principal Business: Petroleum refining
and marketing
Contact: Manager of College Recruiting
Telephone: (216) 586-3467

BRINKS HOME SECURITY, INC.
1628 Valwood Parkway
Carrollton, TX 75006
Principal Business: Marketing of
security systems

Contact: Director of Human Resources
Telephone: (214) 484-1755

BRISTOL-MYERS SQUIBB COMPANY
345 Park Avenue
New York, NY 10154
Principal Business: Manufacturing
and marketing of pharmaceutical and
consumer products
Contact: Corporate Director of
Recruiting

THE BROADWAY
3880 North Mission Road
Los Angeles, CA 90031
Principal Business: Department store
retailing
Contact: Manager of Executive
Development
Telephone: (213) 227-2132

BROWN GROUP, INC.
8400 Maryland Avenue
St. Louis, MO 63166
Principal Business: Manufacturing and
retailing of footwear
Contact: Employment Administrator
Telephone: (314) 854-4000

BROWN SHOE COMPANY
8300 Maryland Avenue
St. Louis, MO 63105
Principal Business: Manufacturing and
marketing of footwear
Contact: Director of Executive
Development & Training
Telephone: (314) 854-2170

BULL HN INFORMATION SYSTEMS
300 Concord Road
Billerica, MA 01821
Principal Business: Designing and
servicing of computer software
Contact: Manager of University
Relations
Telephone: (508) 294-4476

BURGER KING CORPORATION
17777 Old Cutler Road
Miami, FL 33157
Principal Business: Fast-food
franchising
Contact: Manager of Management
Development
Telephone: (305) 378-7831

BURKE MARKETING RESEARCH
Two Centennial Plaza

Cincinnati, OH 45202
Principal Business: Marketing
research and information services
Contact: Professional Recruitment
Telephone: (513) 241-5663

BURLINGTON INDUSTRIES, INC.
3330 West Friendly Avenue
Greensboro, NC 27420
Principal Business: Manufacturing and
marketing of textile products
Contact: Manager of Organization
Planning & Development
Telephone: (919) 379-4588

LEO BURNETT COMPANY, Inc.
35 West Wacker Drive
Chicago, IL 60601
Principal Business: Advertising
services
Contact: Director of Recruiting
Telephone: (312) 220-5959

BURROUGHS WELLCOME COMPANY
3030 Cornwallis Road
Research Triangle Park, NC 27709
Principal Business: Manufacturing and
marketing of pharmaceutical products
Contact: Human Resources Manager
Telephone: (919) 248-4611

CAMPBELL SOUP COMPANY
Campbell Place
Camden, NJ 08101
Principal Business: Manufacturing
and marketing of soup and other food
products
Contact: Recruitment & Staffing
Specialist
Telephone: (609) 342-6295

CARGILL, INC.
P.O. Box 9300
Minnetonka, MN 55440
Principal Business: Processing and
marketing of agricultural and other
commodities
Contact: College Programs Manager
Telephone: (612) 475-7833

CARROLS CORPORATION
3265 West Market Street
Akron, OH 44313
Principal Business: Food service
management
Contact: Personnel Manager
Telephone: (216) 864-9977

CARTER HAWLEY HALE STORES, INC.
444 South Flower Street
Los Angeles, CA 90071
  Principal Business: Department store
  retailing
  Contact: Manager of Executive
  Recruitment
  Telephone: (213) 239-6724

CENTEL CORPORATION
8725 Higgins Road
Chicago, IL 60631
  Principal Business: Telecommuni-
  cations services
  Contact: Human Resource Development
  Telephone: (312) 399-2901

CENTURY 21 REAL ESTATE CORPORATION
2601 Southeast Main Street
Irvine, CA 92713
  Principal Business: Real-estate
  services
  Contact: Director of Career
  Development
  Telephone: (714) 553-2100

CHAMPION INTERNATIONAL CORPORATION
One Champion Plaza
Stamford, CT 06921
  Principal Business: Manufacturing
  and marketing of forest and paper
  products
  Contact: Manager of College Relations
  Telephone: (203) 358-7382

CHASE MANHATTAN BANK
One Chase Manhattan Plaza
New York, NY 10081
  Principal Business: Financial
  services
  Contact: Personnel Department
  Telephone: (212) 552-3374

CHIAT/DAY/MOJO, INC.
340 Main Street
Venice, CA 90291
  Principal Business: Advertising
  services
  Contact: Personnel Department
  Telephone: (310) 314-5000

CHICAGO RAWHIDE MANUFACTURING COMPANY
900 North State Street
Elgin, IL 60123
  Principal Business: Manufacturing and
  marketing of seals, bearings, filter-
  ing devices, and diesel engine parts

  Contact: Manager of Employee
  Relations
  Telephone: (708) 742-7840

CHILTON RESEARCH SERVICES
201 King of Prussia Road
Radnor, PA 19089
  Principal Business: Marketing research
  and information services
  Contact: Personnel Department
  Telephone: (215) 964-4602

CHRYSLER CORPORATION
12000 Chrysler Drive
Highland Park, MI 48288
  Principal Business: Manufacturing and
  marketing of motor vehicles
  Contact: Manager of College Relations &
  Recruiting Programs
  Telephone: (313) 956-1268

CIBA-GEIGY CORPORATION
444 Saw Mill River Road
Ardsley, NY 10502
  Principal Business: Manufacturing and
  marketing of pharmaceuticals, chemicals,
  and other products
  Contact: Recruitment
  Telephone: (914) 479-4054

CIGNA CORPORATION
900 Cottage Grove Road
Bloomfield, CT 06002
  Principal Business: Insurance and other
  financial services
  Contact: Recruitment
  Telephone: (203) 726-5040

CIRCUIT CITY STORES, INC.
9950 Maryland Drive
Richmond, VA 23233
  Principal Business: Consumer electronics
  retailing
  Contact: Manager of Management
  Recruitment

CITIBANK
575 Lexington Avenue
New York, NY 10043
  Principal Business: Financial services
  Contact: Director of Management
  Associate Programs
  Telephone: (212) 559-6507

LIZ CLAIBORNE, INC.
One Claiborne Avenue
North Bergen, NJ 07047
  Principal Business: Manufacturing

and retailing of apparel and related products
Contact: Manager of College Relations
Telephone: (201) 601-7530

C & J CLARK AMERICA, RETAIL DIVISION
520 South Broad Street
Kennett Square, PA 19348
  Principal Business: Manufacturing, wholesaling, and retailing of footwear
  Contact: Director of Training & Recruitment
  Telephone: (215) 444-6550

CLOROX COMPANY
P.O. Box 24305
Oakland, CA 94623
  Principal Business: Manufacturing and marketing of household products
  Contact: Senior College Relations Specialist
  Telephone: (510) 271-7771

COCA-COLA USA
P.O. Drawer 1734
Atlanta, GA 30301
  Principal Business: Manufacturing and marketing of soft drinks
  Contact: Staffing Specialist
  Telephone: (404) 676-7555

CODEX CORPORATION
20 Cabot Boulevard
Mansfield, MA 02048
  Principal Business: Manufacturing and marketing of modems, multiplexors, and network management systems
  Contact: College Relations Manager
  Telephone: (508) 261-4000

COLGATE-PALMOLIVE COMPANY
300 Park Avenue
New York, NY 10022
  Principal Business: Manufacturing and marketing of consumer products
  Contact: Manager of Recruitment & Development
  Telephone: (212) 310-2829

COMPUSERVE INCORPORATED
5000 Arlington Centre Boulevard
Columbus, OH 43220
  Principal Business: Computerized on-line information services
  Contact: Employment Representative
  Telephone: (614) 457-8600

COMPUTER ASSOCIATES INTERNATIONAL, INC.
711 Stewart Avenue
Garden City, NY 11530
  Principal Business: Developing and marketing computer software
  Contact: Personnel Department

COMPUTER LANGUAGE RESEARCH
2395 Midway Road
Carrollton, TX 75006
  Principal Business: Computerized tax returns and electronic forms systems
  Contact: Professional Recruitment
  Telephone: (214) 250-7000

CONAGRA, INC.
One ConAgra Drive
Omaha, NE 68102
  Principal Business: Manufacturing and marketing of food products
  Contact: Personnel Department
  Telephone: (402) 595-4000

CONOCO INC.
P.O. Box 2197
Houston, TX 77252
  Principal Business: Petroleum refining and marketing
  Contact: Supervisor of University Relations & Recruiting
  Telephone: (713) 293-1964

CONTEMPO CASUALS
5433 West Jefferson Boulevard
Los Angeles, CA 90016
  Principal Business: Apparel retailing
  Contact: Director of Human Resources
  Telephone: (213) 930-4660

CONTINENTAL INSURANCE
180 Maiden Lane
New York, NY 10038
  Principal Business: Insurance services
  Contact: Manager of Employee Development
  Telephone: (212) 440-3672

COOPER INDUSTRIES
P.O. Box 4446
Houston, TX 77210
  Principal Business: Manufacturing and marketing of electrical products, equipment, and other products
  Contact: Manager of Professional Recruiting
  Telephone: (713) 739-5427

COOPER TIRE & RUBBER COMPANY
P.O. Box 550

Findlay, OH 45839
  Principal Business: Manufacturing and
  marketing of tires and other rubber
  products
  Contact: Manager of Salaried
  Personnel
  Telephone: (419) 424-4341
COORS BREWING COMPANY
311 10th Street
Golden, CO 80401
  Principal Business: Manufacturing and
  marketing of beer products
  Contact: College Recruiting
  Telephone: (303) 277-5547
CORNING
Houghton Park
Corning, NY 14831
  Principal Business: Manufacturing and
  marketing of glass and glass/ceramic
  products
  Contact: Manager of University
  Relations & External Staffing
  Telephone: (607) 974-8454
COUNTY SEAT STORES, INC.
17950 Preston Road
Dallas, TX 75252
  Principal Business: Apparel retailing
  Contact: Director of Field Human
  Resources & Customer Satisfaction
  Telephone: (214) 248-5231
CRAY RESEARCH, INC.
655D Lone Oak Drive
Eagan, MN 55121
  Principal Business: Manufacturing and
  marketing of scientific computers
  Contact: Director of Staffing
  Telephone: (612) 683-5575
CUMMINS ENGINE COMPANY, INC.
P.O. Box 3005, Mail Code 60808
Columbus, IN 47202
  Principal Business: Manufacturing
  and marketing of diesel engines and
  related components, and power systems
  Contact: Director of Corporate
  Recruiting
  Telephone: (812) 377-3107
HELENE CURTIS, INC.
325 North Wells Street
Chicago, IL 60610
  Principal Business: Manufacturing and
  marketing of personal-care products

  Contact: Employment Manager
CVS/PHARMACY
One CVS Drive
Woonsocket, RI 02895
  Principal Business: Drugstore
  retailing
  Contact: Manager of Recruiting and
  Manpower Planning
  Telephone: (401) 765-1500, Extension
  5265
DAN RIVER, INC.
P.O. Box 261
Danville, VA 24543
  Principal Business: Manufacturing and
  marketing of textile products
  Contact: Director of Employee
  Relations
D'ARCY MASIUS BENTON & BOWLES, INC.
1675 Broadway
New York, NY 10019
  Principal Business: Advertising
  services
  Contact: Personnel Department
  Telephone: (212) 468-3622
DATA GENERAL CORPORATION
4400 Computer Drive
Westborough, MA 01580
  Principal Business: Manufacturing,
  marketing, and servicing of computer
  systems
  Contact: College Relations Manager
  Telephone: (508) 366-8911
DDB NEEDHAM WORLDWIDE, INC.
437 Madison Avenue
New York, NY 10022
  Principal Business: Advertising
  services
  Contact: Personnel Department
  Telephone: (212) 415-2000
DEAN WITTER FINANCIAL SERVICES GROUP
2500 Lake Cook Road
Riverwoods, IL 60015
  Principal Business: Financial
  services
  Contact: Employment Manager
  Telephone: (708) 405-1510
DEERE & COMPANY
John Deere Road
Moline, IL 61265
  Principal Business: Manufacturing and
  marketing of equipment, providing of

financial and other services
Contact: Manager of Recruiting
Telephone: (309) 765-4126

DELCO ELECTRONICS CORPORATION
One Corporate Center
Kokomo, IN 46904
Principal Business: Manufacturing and
marketing of automotive and other
electronics
Contact: Manager of Placement &
College Relations

DELTA AIR LINES
Hartsfield International Airport
Atlanta, GA 30320
Principal Business: Air
transportation
Contact: Personnel Department
Telephone: (404) 715-2600

DELUXE CHECK PRINTERS, INC.
1600 East Touhy Avenue
Des Planes, IL 60018
Principal Business: Manufacturing
and marketing of printed financial
documents
Contact: Recruiting & Development
Telephone: (708) 635-7200

DIEBOLD, INC.
P.O. Box 8230
Canton, OH 44711
Principal Business: Manufacturing,
marketing, and servicing of automatic
transaction systems and security
equipment
Contact: Manager of Salaried
Employment
Telephone: (216) 497-4623

DIGITAL EQUIPMENT CORPORATION
111 Powdermill Road
Maynard, MA 01754
Principal Business: Manufacturing and
marketing of computers and computer
systems
Contact: Manager of U.S. College
Relations
Telephone: (508) 493-9444

WALT DISNEY COMPANY
P.O. Box 10090
Lake Buena Vista, FL 32830
Principal Business: Entertainment
services
Contact: Manager of College Relations

Telephone: (407) 828-3092

DIVERSEY CORPORATION
1532 Biddle Avenue
Wyandotte, MI 48192
Principal Business: Manufacturing and
marketing of specialty chemicals and
designing of equipment
Contact: Manager of Staffing and
Personnel Administration
Telephone: (313) 281-0930

THE DOCTORS' COMPANY
P.O. Box 2900
1127 First Street
Napa, CA 94558
Principal Business: Medical
malpractice insurance services
Contact: Human Resource Specialist

DOLE PACKAGED FOODS COMPANY
50 California Street
San Francisco, CA 94111
Principal Business: Producing and
marketing fruit-based products
Contact: Manager of Employee
Relations
Telephone: (415) 986-3000

DOMINO'S PIZZA
30 Frank Lloyd Wright Drive
P.O. Box 997
Ann Arbor, MI 48106
Principal business: Fast-food
franchising
Contact: National Manager of
Recruiting
Telephone: (313) 930-4456

R. R. DONNELLEY & SONS COMPANY
2223 Martin Luther King Drive
Chicago, IL 60616
Principal Business: Printing and
marketing of books, magazines,
catalogs, directories, documents,
computer software and hardware
documentation, and data bases
Contact: Human Resources Manager
Telephone: (312) 326-8048

DOVER ELEVATOR SYSTEMS, INC.
P.O. Box 2177
Memphis, TN 38101
Principal Business: Manufacturing and
marketing of elevators and lifting
equipment
Contact: Human Resources/EEO Manager

Telephone: (601) 393-2110

DOW CHEMICAL, U.S.A.
Employee Development Center
Midland, MI 48674
    Principal Business: Manufacturing and
    marketing of chemicals, plastics,
    metals, and other products
    Contact: Manager of Recruiting
    Programs
    Telephone: (517) 636-2177

DOW CORNING CORPORATION
2200 West Salzburg Road
Midland, MI 48686
    Principal Business: Manufacturing and
    marketing of silicone-based products
    Contact: Manager of Employment Center
    Telephone: (517) 496-8185

DRACKETT COMPANY
201 East Fourth Street
Cincinnati, OH 45202
    Principal Business: Manufacturing
    and marketing of household cleaning
    products
    Contact: Director of Human Resources
    Telephone: (513) 632-1807

DUN'S MARKETING SERVICES
Three Sylvan Way
Parsippany, NJ 07054
    Principal Business: Business
    information services
    Contact: Recruiting Coordinator
    Telephone: (201) 455-0900

E. I. DU PONT DE NEMOURS AND COMPANY
1007 Market Street
Wilmington, DE 19898
    Principal Business: Manufacturing and
    marketing of chemical, fiber, film,
    resin, energy, and other products
    Contact: Manager of Staffing
    Telephone: (302) 774-4651

EASTMAN CHEMICAL COMPANY
P.O. Box 1975
Kingsport, TN 37662
    Principal Business: Manufacturing and
    marketing of chemicals, fibers, and
    plastics
    Contact: Employment Manager
    Telephone: (615) 229-3111

EASTMAN KODAK COMPANY
343 State Street
Rochester, NY 14650
    Principal Business: Diversified
    manufacturing and marketing
    Contact: Director of Corporate
    Professional Recruitment & University
    Development
    Telephone: (716) 724-2111

EATON CORPORATION
Eaton Center
Cleveland, OH 44114
    Principal Business: Manufacturing and
    marketing of advanced technology
    products
    Contact: Manager of Appraisal and
    Staffing
    Telephone: (216) 523-4355

ECKERD DRUG COMPANY
8333 Bryan Dairy Road
Clearwater, FL 34618
    Principal Business: Drugstore
    retailing
    Contact: Recruiting & Staffing
    Specialist
    Telephone: (813) 397-7461

EDISON BROTHERS STORES, INC.
501 North Broadway
St. Louis, MO 63102
    Principal Business: Footwear and
    apparel retailing
    Contact: Assistant Sales Training
    Director
    Telephone: (314) 331-6994

ELECTRONIC DATA SYSTEMS CORPORATION
Suite 200
12200 Park Central Drive
Dallas, TX 75251
    Principal Business: Management
    information systems services
    Contact: Campus Relations
    Telephone: (214) 715-1100

EMERSON POWER TRANSMISSION CORPORATION
620 South Aurora Street
Ithaca, NY 14850
    Principal Business: Manufacturing and
    marketing of electrical/mechanical
    components
    Contact: Director of Sales Training
    Telephone: (607) 272-7220, Extension
    6105

ENGELHARD CORPORATION
101 Wood Avenue
Iselin, NJ 08830

Principal Business: Manufacturing and
marketing of specialty chemicals and
engineered materials
Contact: Manager of Human Resources
Telephone: (908) 205-7091

EQUIFAX, INC.
P.O. Box 4081
Atlanta, GA 30302
Principal Business: Consumer
credit-information services
Contact: Director of Corporate
Employment
Telephone: (404) 885-8160

ERIE INSURANCE GROUP
100 Erie Insurance Place
Erie, PA 16530
Principal Business: Insurance and
other financial services
Contact: Employment Manager
Telephone: (814) 870-2000

EVEREADY BATTERY COMPANY, INC.
25225 Detroit Road
Westlake, OH 44145
Principal Business: Manufacturing and
marketing of batteries and lighting
products
Contact: Manager of Recruiting
Telephone: (216) 835-7826

EXXON CORPORATION
P.O. Box 2180
Houston, TX 77252
Principal Business: Petroleum
refining and marketing
Contact: Coordinator of Professional
Employment
Telephone: (713) 656-4454

FIELDCREST CANNON, INC.
P.O. Box 27054
Greensboro, NC 27425
Principal Business: Manufacturing and
marketing of textile products
Contact: Manager of Management
Employment & Development
Telephone: (919) 665-4359

FILENE'S
426 Washington Street
Boston, MA 02101
Principal Business: Department store
retailing
Contact: Manager of Executive
Recruitment & College Relations

Telephone: (617) 357-2085

FINGERHUT CORPORATION
4400 Baker Road
Minnetonka, MN 55343
Principal: Direct marketing of
consumer products
Contact: Senior Human Resources
Representative
Telephone: (612) 932-3239

FIREMAN'S FUND INSURANCE COMPANY
1600 Los Gamos Drive
San Rafael, CA 94911
Primary Business: Insurance services
Contact: College Relations
Telephone: (415) 492-5000

FIRST BRANDS CORPORATION
88 Long Hill Street
East Hartford, CT 06128
Primary Business: Manufacturing and
marketing of consumer products
Contact: Manager of Employee
Relations
Telephone: (203) 728-6000, Extension
6146

FIRST NATIONAL SUPERMARKETS, INC.
500 North Street
Windsor Locks, CT 06096
Principal Business: Supermarket
retailing
Contact: Manager of Recruitment &
College Affairs
Telephone: (203) 627-2351

FIRST UNION CORPORATION
1400 One First Union Center
Charlotte, NC 28288
Principal Business: Financial
services
Contact: Manager of College
Recruiting
Telephone: (704) 374-2410

FMC CORPORATION
200 East Randolph Drive
Chicago, IL 60601
Principal Business: Manufacturing and
marketing of machinery and chemicals
Contact: University Relations
Supervisor
Telephone: (312) 861-6409

FOLEY'S
P.O. Box 1971
Houston, TX 77251

Principal Business: Department store
retailing
Contact: Manager of Executive
Recruitment & Placement
Telephone: (713) 651-6557

FOOTE, CONE & BELDING COMMUNICATIONS
101 East Erie Street
Chicago, IL 60611
Principal Business: Advertising
services
Contact: Personnel Department
Telephone: (312) 751-7000

FORD MOTOR COMPANY
American Road
World Headquarters
Dearborn, MI 48121
Principal Business: Manufacturing and
marketing of motor vehicles
Contact: Manager of College
Recruiting & Central Placement
Services
Telephone: (313) 322-7500

FORD NEW HOLLAND, INC.
500 Diller Avenue
New Holland, PA 17557
Principal Business: Manufacturing and
marketing of agricultural equipment
Contact: Recruitment & Placement
Manager
Telephone: (717) 355-4036

FORMOSA PLASTICS CORPORATION, U.S.A.
9 Peach Tree Hill Road
Livingston, NJ 07039
Principal Business: Manufacturing and
marketing of petrochemicals
Contact: Corporate Personnel Director
Telephone: (201) 966-6980, Extension
250

FRANK'S NURSERY & CRAFTS, INC.
6501 East Nevada
Detroit, MI 48234
Principal Business: Lawn and garden
products retailing
Contact: Manager of Human Resources
Telephone: (313) 366-8400

FRITO-LAY, INC.
7701 Legacy Drive
Plano, TX 75024
Principal Business: Manufacturing and
marketing of snack foods
Contact: Group Manager of Staffing

Telephone: (214) 353-2379
FRUEHAUF TRAILER CORPORATION
26999 Central Park Boulevard
Southfield, MI 48076
Principal Business: Manufacturing and
marketing of truck trailers
Contact: Manager of Personnel and
Benefits

FURR'S/BISHOP'S INCORPORATED
P.O. Box 6747
Lubbock, TX 79493
Principal Business: Cafeteria and
restaurant retailing
Contact: Recruitment
Telephone: (806) 792-7151, Extension
304

E. & J. GALLO WINERY
P.O. Box 1130
Modesto, CA 95353
Principal Business: Manufacturing and
marketing of wines and brandy
Contact: Director of Sales Personnel
Telephone: (209) 579-3795

GAST MANUFACTURING CORPORATION
P.O. Box 97
Benton Harbor, MI 49022
Principal Business: Manufacturing and
marketing of compressors, pumps, and
air motors
Contact: Director of Industrial
Relations and Personnel

GEHL COMPANY
143 East Water Street
West Bend, WI 53095
Principal Business: Manufacturing and
marketing of farm machinery and other
equipment
Contact: Manager of Recruitment and
Employee Development

GENERAL DYNAMICS CORPORATION
3190 Fairview Park Drive
Falls Church, VA 22042
Principal Business: Manufacturing and
marketing of aerospace and building
products
Contact: Corporate Director of
Executive Staffing

GENERAL ELECTRIC COMPANY
1285 Boston Avenue
Bridgeport, CT 06601
Principal Business: Diversified

CHAPTER FOUR: FIRMS WITH MARKETING-RELATED POSITIONS

manufacturing and services
Contact: Manager of Recruiting &
University Development
Telephone: (203) 382-3071

GENERAL MILLS, INC.
P.O. Box 1113
Minneapolis, MN 55440
Principal Business: Manufacturing
and marketing of consumer foods, and
restaurant retailing
Contact: Director of Recruitment &
College Relations
Telephone: (612) 540-7504

GENERAL MOTORS CORPORATION
3044 West Grand Boulevard
Detroit, MI 48202
Principal Business: Manufacturing and
marketing of motor vehicles
Contact: Assistant Director of
College Relations
Telephone: (313) 556-3569

GENERAL TIRE, INC.
One General Street
Akron, OH 44329
Principal Business: Manufacturing and
marketing of tires
Contact: Director of Human Resource
Development & Training
Telephone: (216) 798-2437

GEORGIA-PACIFIC CORPORATION
133 Peachtree Street, Northeast
Atlanta, GA 30303
Principal Business: Manufacturing and
marketing of forest products
Contact: Manager of Employment &
College Relations
Telephone: (404) 521-4024

GILLETTE COMPANY
Prudential Tower Building
Boston, MA 02199
Principal Business: Manufacturing and
marketing of consumer products
Contact: College Relations Supervisor
Telephone: (617) 421-7658

GLAXO, INC.
Five Moore Drive
P.O. Box 13398
Research Triangle Park, NC 27709
Principal Business: Manufacturing and
marketing of pharmaceutical products
Contact: Manager of Human Resources

Telephone: (919) 248-2394

GLIDDEN COMPANY
925 Euclid Avenue
Cleveland, OH 44115
Principal Business: Manufacturing and
marketing of paint
Contact: Supervisor of Employment
Telephone: (216) 344-8105

GOLD KIST, INC.
P.O. Box 2210
Atlanta, GA 30301
Principal Business: Manufacturing and
marketing of farm production supplies
Contact: Director of Human Resources
Planning & Employment
Telephone: (404) 393-5249

BF GOODRICH COMPANY
3925 Embassy Parkway
Akron, OH 44313
Principal Business: Manufacturing
and marketing of vinyl resins and
compounds, plastics, specialty
chemicals, and other products
Contact: Manager of Human Resources
Telephone: (216) 374-2144

GOODYEAR TIRE & RUBBER COMPANY
1144 East Market Street
Akron, OH 44316
Principal Business: Manufacturing
and marketing of tires and rubber,
chemical, and plastic products
Contact: Manager of Corporate College
Relations
Telephone: (216) 796-7990

E. GOTTSCHALK & COMPANY, INC.
860 Fulton Street
Fresno, CA 93721
Principal Business: Department store
retailing
Contact: Director of Training &
Recruitment
Telephone: (209) 488-7311

W. R. GRACE & CO.
One Town Center Drive
Boca Raton, FL 33486
Principal Business: Manufacturing and
marketing of specialty chemicals
Contact: Director of Employee
Relations
Telephone: (407) 362-2310

GRAINGER

333 Knightsbridge Parkway
Lincolnshire, IL 60069
  Principal Business: Marketing of
  electrical and mechanical equipment,
  components, and supplies
  Contact: Area Personnel Manager of
  Field Operations
  Telephone: (708) 913-8333

GREAT ATLANTIC & PACIFIC TEA COMPANY
2 Paragon Drive
Montvale, NJ 07645
  Principal Business: Supermarket
  retailing
  Contact: Manager of Personnel and
  Employment
  Telephone: (201) 930-4416

GREY ADVERTISING, INC.
777 Third Avenue
New York, NY 10017
  Principal Business: Advertising
  services
  Contact: Associate Director of
  Personnel
  Telephone: (212) 546-2000

GTE CORPORATION
One Stamford Forum
Stamford, CT 06904
  Principal Business: Telecommuni-
  cations services
  Contact: Manager of College Relations
  Telephone: (203) 965-3454

GULF POWER COMPANY
P.O. Box 1151
Pensacola, FL 32520
  Principal Business: Electric utility
  services
  Contact: Supervisor of Employment
  Telephone: (904) 444-5481

HAGGAR APPAREL COMPANY
6113 Lemmon Avenue
Dallas, TX 75209
  Principal Business: Manufacturing and
  marketing of apparel
  Contact: Vice-President of Human
  Resources
  Telephone: (214) 956-0424

HALLMARK CARDS, INC.
2501 McGee Trafficway
P.O. Box 419580
Kansas City, MO 64141
  Principal Business: Publishing and

marketing of personal expression
products
  Contact: Manager of College Relations
  Telephone: (816) 274-8512

JOHN HANCOCK MUTUAL LIFE INSURANCE COMPANY
197 Clarendon Street
P.O. Box 111
Boston, MA 02117
  Principal Business: Insurance and
  other financial services
  Contact: Coordinator of College
  Recruiting
  Telephone: (617) 572-4503

HARLEY-DAVIDSON, INC.
3700 Juneau Avenue
Milwaukee, WI 53208
  Principal Business: Manufacturing
  and marketing of motorcycles and
  recreational vehicles
  Contact: Human Resources Specialist
  Telephone: (414) 935-4045

HARRIS CORPORATION
1025 West NASA Boulevard
Melbourne, FL 32919
  Principal Business: Manufacturing and
  marketing of electronic systems,
  semiconductors, and office equipment
  Contact: Supervisor of Human
  Resources
  Telephone: (407) 724-3410

HASBRO, INC.
200 Narragansett Park Drive
Pawtucket, RI 02861
  Principal Business: Manufacturing and
  marketing of toys and games
  Contact: Director of College
  Recruiting
  Telephone: (401) 431-8697

HAWORTH, INC.
One Haworth Center
Holland, MI 49423
  Principal Business: Manufacturing and
  marketing of office furniture
  Contact: Manager of Staffing and
  Placement
  Telephone: (616) 393-1051

HECHT'S DEPARTMENT STORES
685 North Glebe Road
Arlington, VA 22203
  Principal Business: Department store

retailing
Contact: Manager of Executive
Recruiting & Placement
Telephone: (703) 558-1612

H. J. HEINZ COMPANY
600 Grant Street
Pittsburgh, PA 15230
Principal Business: Manufacturing and
marketing of food products
Contact: Personnel Department
Telephone: (412) 456-5700

HENKELS & McCOY, INC.
985 Jolly Road
Blue Bell, PA 19422
Principal Business: Telecommunica-
tions and pipeline construction
Contact: Senior Director of Human
Resources
Telephone: (215) 283-7688

HERCULES INCORPORATED
Hercules Plaza
Wilmington, DE 19894
Principal Business: Manufacturing
and marketing of specialty and
intermediate chemicals
Contact: Manager of Professional
Staffing & College Relations
Telephone: (302) 594-6030

HERSHEY CHOCOLATE U.S.A.
14 East Chocolate Avenue
Hershey, PA 17033
Principal Business: Manufacturing
and marketing of chocolate and
confectionery products
Contact: Director of Human Resources
Telephone: (717) 534-7909

HESS'S DEPARTMENT STORES, INC.
Hamilton Mall at Ninth Street
Allentown, PA 18101
Principal Business: Department store
retailing
Contact: Assistant Executive Director
of Personnel
Telephone: (215) 821-5266

HEUBLEIN, INC.
16 Munson Road
Farmington, CT 06032
Principal Business: Manufacturing and
marketing of alcoholic beverages
Contact: Manager of Staffing
Telephone: (203) 678-6562

HEWLETT-PACKARD COMPANY
3000 Hanover Street
MS-20AC
Palo Alto, CA 94304
Principal Business: Manufacturing
and marketing of computers, test and
measuring instruments, and laser
printers
Contact: Recruiting Coordinator
Telephone: (415) 857-2347

HFSI
7900 Westpark Drive
McLean, VA 22102
Principal Business: Developing and
marketing of information systems
Contact: Manager of Employment
Programs
Telephone: (703) 827-3281

HILLS DEPARTMENT STORES
15 Dan Road
Canton, MA 02021
Principal Business: Discount
department-store retailing
Contact: Assistant Vice-President for
Employment & Benefits
Telephone: (617) 821-1000

HILTON HOTELS CORPORATION
9336 Civic Center Drive
Beverly Hills, CA 90209
Principal Business: Hotel and casino
services
Contact: Director of Recruitment
Telephone: (213) 205-4322

HOECHST CELANESE CORPORATION
Route 202-206 North
P.O. Box 2500
Somerville, NJ 08876
Principal Business: Manufacturing and
marketing of chemical products
Contact: Director of University
Recruiting
Telephone: (201) 231-4861

HONEYWELL, INC.
Honeywell Plaza
Minneapolis, MN 55408
Principal Business: Manufacturing
and marketing of advanced-technology
products
Contact: Corporate Manager of
Staffing & University Relations
Telephone: (612) 870-2160

HOOVER COMPANY
101 East Maple Street
North Canton, OH 44720
  Principal Business: Manufacturing and
  marketing of floor-care products
  Contact: Manager of Human Resources
  Telephone: (216) 499-9200, Extension
  2734

GEO. A. HORMEL & COMPANY
P.O. Box 800
Austin, MN 55912
  Principal Business: Manufacturing and
  marketing of food products
  Contact: Supervisor of Professional
  Employment
  Telephone: (507) 437-5881

HOUSTON'S RESTAURANTS, INC.
8 Piedmont Center
Suite 720
Atlanta, GA 30305
  Principal Business: Restaurant
  retailing
  Contact: Director of Recruiting
  Telephone: (404) 231-0161

HUNTINGTON NATIONAL BANK
Huntington Center
HC 0344
Columbus, OH 43287
  Principal Business: Financial
  services
  Contact: Management Recruiter
  Telephone: (614) 463-4639

HUNT-WESSON, INC.
1645 West Valencia Drive
Fullerton, CA 92633
  Principal Business: Manufacturing and
  marketing of food products
  Contact: Director of Personnel
  Telephone: (714) 680-1000

HYATT HOTELS CORPORATION
200 West Madison
Chicago, IL 60606
  Principal Business: Hotel services
  Contact: Manager of College Relations
  Telephone: (312) 750-1234

IBM CORPORATION
2000 Purchase Street
Purchase, NY 10577
  Principal Business: Manufacturing and
  marketing of computers and related
  services

Contact: Manager of National College
Recruiting
Telephone: (914) 697-6724

ICI AMERICAS, INC.
Concord Pike and New Murphy Road
Wilmington, DE 19897
  Principal Business: Manufacturing and
  marketing of specialty chemicals,
  pharmaceuticals, and other products
  Contact: Coordinator of College
  Relations
  Telephone: (302) 886-3146

INCO ALLOYS INTERNATIONAL, INC.
P.O. Box 1958
Huntington, WV 25720
  Principal Business: Manufacturing and
  marketing of nickel and nickel alloy
  Contact: Manager of Employment and
  Benefits
  Telephone: (304) 526-5413

INFORMATION RESOURCES, INC.
150 North Clinton Street
Chicago, II 60661
  Principal Business: Marketing
  research and information services
  Contact: Employment Manager
  Telephone: (312) 726-1221

INGERSOLL-RAND COMPANY
200 Chestnut Ridge Road
Woodcliff Lake, NJ 07675
  Principal Business: Manufacturing and
  marketing of industrial machinery and
  related products
  Contact: Manager of College Relations
  Telephone: (201) 573-3304

INTEL CORPORATION
1900 Prairie City Road
Folsom, CA 95630
  Principal Business: Manufacturing and
  marketing of computer components
  (such as central processing units)
  Contact: Corporate Manager of College
  Recruitment
  Telephone: (916) 351-6741

INTERNATIONAL PAPER
6400 Poplar Avenue
Memphis, TN 38197
  Principal Business: Manufacturing and
  marketing of pulp and paper products
  Contact: Supervisor of Corporate
  Recruiting

Telephone: (901) 763-5892

INTERNATIONAL TECHNOLOGY CORPORATION

2790 Mosside Boulevard

Monroeville, PA 15146

Principal Business: Technical consulting services

Contact: Manager of Professional Staffing and College Relations

ITT HARTFORD INSURANCE GROUP

690 Asylum Avenue

Hartford, CT 06115

Principal Business: Insurance services

Contact: Manager of College Relations

Telephone: (203) 547-3943

ITT SHERATON CORPORATION

60 State Street

Boston, MA 02109

Principal Business: Hotel services

Contact: Manager of College Relations

Telephone: (617) 367-3600

JEWEL FOOD STORES

1955 West North Avenue

Melrose Park, IL 60160

Principal Business: Supermarket retailing

Contact: Vice-President of Personnel

Telephone: (708) 531-6949

JOHNSON & JOHNSON

One Johnson & Johnson Plaza

New Brunswick, NJ 08933

Principal Business: Manufacturing and marketing of consumer, pharmaceutical, and health-care products

Contact: Manager of Corporate Search and College Relations

Telephone: (201) 524-3451

S. C. JOHNSON & SON

1525 Howe Street

Racine, WI 53403

Principal Business: Manufacturing and marketing of household products

Contact: Personnel Department

Telephone: (414) 631-2000

K MART CORPORATION

3100 West Big Beaver Road

Troy, MI 48084

Principal Business: Discount department-store retailing

Contact: Senior Director of Field Human Resources

Telephone: (313) 643-1670

KAUFMANN'S DEPARTMENT STORE

400 Fifth Avenue

Pittsburgh, PA 15219

Principal Business: Department store retailing

Contact: Executive Recruitment & Placement

KELLOGG COMPANY

One Kellogg Square

P.O. Box 3599

Battle Creek, MI 49016

Principal Business: Manufacturing and marketing of cereal and other food products

Contact: Corporate Employment Services

Telephone: (616) 961-2405

KETCHUM COMMUNICATIONS, INC.

6 PPG Place

Pittsburgh, PA 15222

Principal Business: Advertising services

Contact: Personnel Department

Telephone: (412) 456-3500

KIMBERLY-CLARK CORPORATION

401 North Lake Street

Neenah, Wl 54956

Principal Business: Manufacturing and marketing of personal-care products

Contact: Recruiting Department

Telephone: (414) 721-2602

KINNEY SHOE CORPORATION

233 Broadway

New York, NY 10279

Principal Business: Manufacturing and retailing of footwear

Contact: Director of Retail Recruiting

Telephone: (212) 720-3987

KNAPP COMMUNICATIONS CORPORATION

5900 Wilshire Boulevard

Los Angeles, CA 90036

Principal Business: Publishing and marketing of magazines

Contact: Supervisor of Compensation, Employment, and Transportation

Telephone: (213) 965-3434

KNIGHT-RIDDER, INC.

One Herald Plaza

Miami, FL 33132

Principal Business: Publishing and
marketing of newspapers and business
information services
Contact: Assistant Vice-President of
Personnel
Telephone: (305) 376-3933

KNOTT'S BERRY FARM
8039 Beach Boulevard
Buena Park, CA 90620
Principal Business: Entertainment and
food services
Contact: Senior Employment
Representative
Telephone: (714) 220-5170

KOHLER COMPANY
444 Highland Drive
Kohler, WI 53044
Principal Business: Manufacturing
and marketing of plumbing and other
products
Contact: Director of Personnel
Telephone: (414) 457-4441, Extension
7367

KOHL'S DEPARTMENT STORES
N54 West 13600 Woodale Drive
Menomonee Falls, WI 53051
Principal Business: Department store
retailing
Contact: Director of Recruiting &
Placement
Telephone: (414) 783-1605

KRAFT GENERAL FOODS
One Kraft Court
Glenview, IL 60025
Principal Business: Manufacturing and
marketing of food products
Contact: Manager of Staffing &
Organization
Telephone: (708) 998-4356

LADY FOOT LOCKER
233 Broadway
New York, NY 10279
Principal Business: Footwear
retailing
Contact: Administrator of Sales &
Personnel
Telephone: (212) 720-3848

LANIER WORLDWIDE, INC.
2300 Parklake Drive, Northeast
Atlanta, GA 30345
Principal Business: Manufacturing

and marketing of automated office
products
Contact: Director of Human Resources
Telephone: (404) 496-9500

LAZARUS DEPARTMENT STORES
699 Race Street
Cincinnati, OH 45202
Principal Business: Department store
retailing
Contact: Corporate College Relations
Manager
Telephone: (513) 369-3403

LEVI STRAUSS & COMPANY
Levi's Plaza
1155 Battery Street
San Francisco, CA 94111
Principal Business: Manufacturing and
marketing of apparel products
Contact: Personnel Department
Telephone: (415) 544-6000

LIBBEY-OWENS-FORD COMPANY
811 Madison Avenue
Toledo, OH 43695
Principal Business: Manufacturing and
marketing of glass products
Contact: Employee Selection
Specialist
Telephone: (419) 247-4534

LIBERTY MUTUAL INSURANCE GROUP
175 Berkeley Street
Boston, MA 02117
Principal Business: Insurance
services
Contact: Director of College
Relations & Placement
Telephone: (617) 357-9500, Extension
43503

ELI LILLY AND COMPANY
Lilly Corporate Center
Indianapolis, IN 46285
Principal Business: Manufacturing and
marketing of pharmaceutical and other
health-care products
Contact: Manager of Professional
Recruitment
Telephone: (317) 276-1050

THE LIMITED STORES, INC.
Three Limited Parkway
P.O. Box 16528
Columbus, OH 43216
Principal Business: Apparel retailing

Contact: Personnel Manager--Stores
Telephone: (614) 479-2000

THOMAS J. LIPTON COMPANY
800 Sylvan Avenue
Englewood Cliffs, NJ 07632
 Principal Business: Manufacturing and
 marketing of food products
 Contact: Personnel Manager of Sales
 Division
 Telephone: (201) 894-7357

LORD & TAYLOR
424 Fifth Avenue
New York, NY 10018
 Principal Business: Department store
 retailing
 Contact: Director of Executive
 Recruitment
 Telephone: (212) 391-3786

LTV STEEL COMPANY
P.O. Box 6778
Cleveland, OH 44101
 Principal Business: Manufacturing and
 marketing of steel and steel products
 Contact: Manager of Human Resources
 Telephone: (216) 622-5270

LUBRIZOL CORPORATION
29400 Lakeland Boulevard
Wickliffe, OH 44092
 Principal Business: Manufacturing and
 marketing of specialty chemicals
 Contact: College Relations
 Coordinator
 Telephone: (216) 943-1200, Extension
 2038

MACK TRUCKS, INC.
Box M
Allentown, PA 18105
 Principal Business: Manufacturing
 and marketing of heavy-duty motor
 vehicles
 Contact: Manager of Employment &
 Training
 Telephone: (215) 439-2205

R. H. MACY & COMPANY, INC.
151 West 34th Street
New York, NY 10001
 Principal Business: Department and
 specialty-store retailing
 Contact: Manager of Executive
 Development
 Telephone: (212) 560-3868

MANVILLE CORPORATION
P.O. Box 5108
Denver, CO 80217
 Principal Business: Manufacturing and
 marketing of paper, wood, packaging,
 fiberglass, and other products
 Contact: Manager of Corporate Human
 Resources
 Telephone: (303) 978-2063

MARATHON OIL COMPANY
539 South Main Street
Findlay, OH 45840
 Principal Business: Petroleum
 refining and marketing
 Contact: Manager of Corporate
 Recruiting
 Telephone: (419) 422-2121

MARION MERRELL DOW, INC.
P.O. Box 9627
Kansas City, MO 64134
 Principal Business: Manufacturing and
 marketing of pharmaceutical products
 Contact: Director of Staffing &
 Relocation
 Telephone: (816) 966-5000

MARITZ MARKETING RESEARCH, INC.
1297 North Highway Drive
Fenton, MO 63099
 Principal Business: Marketing
 research and information services
 Contact: Personnel Department
 Telephone: (314) 827-1610

MARKEM CORPORATION
150 Congress Street
Keene, NH 03431
 Principal Business: Manufacturing and
 marketing of printing systems, inks,
 and chemical products
 Contact: Benefits/Recruitment Manager
 Telephone: (603) 352-1130

MARKET FACTS, INC.
3040 West Salt Creek Lane
Arlington Heights, IL 6004
 Principal Business: Marketing
 research and information services
 Contact: Personnel Department
 Telephone: (708) 590-7000

MARRIOTT CORPORATION
One Marriott Drive
Washington, DC 20058
 Principal Business: Hotel and food

services
Contact: Manager of National
Employment Marketing
Telephone: (301) 380-9000

MARS, INC.
800 High Street
Hackettstown, NJ 07840
Principal Business: Manufacturing and
marketing of food products
Contact: Manager of University
Employment & Relations
Telephone: (201) 852-1000

MARSHALL'S
200 Brickstone Square
P.O. Box 9030
Andover, MA 01810
Principal Business: Apparel Retailing
Contact: Personnel Manager
Telephone: (508) 474-7000

MASSEY-FERGUSON, INC.
P.O. Box 1813
Des Moines, IA 50306
Principal Business: Marketing of farm
equipment
Contact: Human Resources Manager

MATTEL TOYS, INC.
333 Continental Boulevard
El Segundo, CA 90245
Principal Business: Manufacturing and
marketing of toys
Contact: Director of Recruitment
Telephone: (213) 524-3532

TJ MAXX
770 Cochituate Road
Framingham, MA 01701
Principal Business: Apparel retailing
Contact: Vice-President for
Recruiting
Telephone: (508) 390-3398

MAY DEPARTMENT STORES COMPANY
611 Olive Street
St. Louis, MO 63101
Principal Business: Department and
specialty-store retailing
Contact: Director of Executive
Recruiting
Telephone: (314) 342-6778

MAYBELLINE, INC.
3030 Jackson Avenue
Memphis, TN 38112
Principal Business: Manufacturing and

marketing of cosmetics
Contact: Supervisor of Human
Resources

OSCAR MAYER FOODS CORPORATION
910 Mayer Avenue
Madison, WI 53704
Principal Business: Manufacturing and
marketing of food products
Contact: Manager of University
Relations
Telephone: (608) 241-3311

MAYTAG COMPANY
One Dependability Square
Newton, IA 50208
Principal Business: Manufacturing and
marketing of appliances
Contact: Manager of Staffing
Telephone: (515) 791-8288

THOM McAN SHOE COMPANY
67 Millbrook Street
Worcester, MA 01606
Principal Business: Footwear retailing
Contact: Vice-President of Human
Resources
Telephone: (508) 791-3811, Extension 430

McCANN-ERICKSON WORLDWIDE
750 Third Avenue
New York, NY 10017
Principal Business: Advertising
services
Contact: Personnel Department
Telephone: (212) 697-6000

McCORMICK & COMPANY, INC.
10950 Beaver Dam Road
Hunt Valley, MD 21030
Principal Business: Manufacturing
and manufacturing of seasoning,
flavoring, and other food products
Contact: Human Relations Manager
Telephone: (301) 771-7595

McCRORY STORES
2955 East Market Street
York, PA 17402
Principal Business: Variety store
retailing
Contact: Director of Personnel
Operations
Telephone: (717) 757-8262

McCULLOCH CORPORATION
P.O. Box 11990
Tucson, AZ 85734

Principal Business: Manufacturing and
marketing of chain saws, engines, and
lawn and garden products
Contact: Human Resources
Telephone: (602) 574-1311

McDONALD'S RESTAURANT CORPORATION
Kroc Drive
Oak Brook, IL 60521
Primary Business: Fast-food
franchising
Contact: National Personnel
Department

MCI TELECOMMUNICATIONS
601 South 12th Street
Arlington, VA 22202
Principal Business: Telecommunica-
ions services
Contact: College Relations
Coordinator
Telephone: (703) 486-6067

McNEIL CONSUMER PRODUCTS COMPANY
Camp Hill Road
Fort Washington, PA 19034
Principal Business: Manufacturing
and marketing of over-the-counter
analgesic products
Contact: Senior Employment
Administrator

MEAD CORPORATION
Courthouse Plaza, Northeast
Dayton, OH 45463
Principal Business: Manufacturing and
marketing of pulp, paper, and other
products and services
Contact: Manager of College Recruit-
ing & Relations
Telephone: (513) 495-4092

MEDTRONIC, INC.
7000 Central Avenue, Northeast
Minneapolis, MN 55432
Principal Business: Manufacturing
and marketing of therapeutic medical
devices
Contact: Corporate Employment Manager
Telephone: (612) 574-3705

MEIJER, INC.
2727 Walker Northwest
Grand Rapids, MI 49504
Principal Business: Food and general
merchandise retailing
Contact: Senior Recruiter

Telephone: (616) 791-5216

MERCANTILE STORES COMPANY, INC.
128 West 31st Street
New York, NY 10001
Principal Business: Department store
retailing
Contact: Manager of Personnel/
Operations
Telephone: (212) 560-0287

MERCK & COMPANY, INC.
P.O. Box 2000
Rahway, NJ 07065
Principal Business: Manufacturing and
marketing of health-care products and
specialty chemicals.
Contact: Manager of College Relations
Telephone: (908) 594-6221

MERIDIAN BANCORP, INC.
35 North Sixth Street
P.O. Box 1102
Reading, PA 19603
Principal Business: Financial
services
Contact: Human Resources Officer
Telephone: (215) 854-3015

MERRILL LYNCH & COMPANY, INC.
250 Vesey Street
New York, NY 10281
Principal Business: Financial
services
Contact: Director of Recruiting
Telephone: (212) 449-9836

MERVYN'S
25001 Industrial Boulevard
Hayward, CA 94545
Principal Business: Department store
retailing
Contact: College Relations
Representative
Telephone: (415) 786-8810

**METROPOLITAN LIFE AND AFFILIATED
COMPANIES**
One Madison Avenue
New York, NY 10010
Principal Business: Insurance and
other financial services
Contact: College Relations Consultant
Telephone: (212) 578-5592

MICHELIN TIRE CORPORATION, USA
P.O. Box 19001
Greenville, SC 29602

Principal Business: Manufacturing and marketing of tires
Contact: Director of Recruiting
Telephone: (803) 458-5000, Extension 5286

MICHIGAN BELL TELEPHONE COMPANY
444 Michigan Avenue
Detroit, MI 48226
Principal Business: Telecommunications services and equipment
Contact: Assistant Director of Employment

MICROSOFT CORPORATION
One Microsoft Way
Redmond, WA 98052
Principal Business: Developing and marketing of computer software
Contact: College Relations Manager
Telephone: (206) 867-3010

MILLER BREWING COMPANY
3939 West Highland Boulevard
Milwaukee, WI 53201
Principal Business: Manufacturing and marketing of beer
Contact: Sales and Marketing Recruiter
Telephone: (414) 931-2253

MILLIKEN & COMPANY
P.O. Box 1926
M260
Spartanburg, SC 29304
Principal Business: Manufacturing and marketing of textiles
Contact: Director of College Relations
Telephone: (803) 573-2508

MOBIL CORPORATION
3225 Gallows Road
Fairfax, VA 22037
Principal Business: Petroleum refining and marketing
Contact: Manager of Recruiting Operations
Telephone: (703) 846-3637

MONARCH MARKING
Monarch Lane
Miamisburg, OH 45342
Principal Business: Manufacturing and marketing of price-marking supplies and equipment, and product identification items

Contact: Manager of Employment
Telephone: (513) 865-2548

MONSANTO COMPANY
800 North Lindbergh Boulevard
St. Louis, MO 63167
Principal Business: Diversified manufacturing and marketing
Contact: Director of University Relations
Telephone: (314) 694-2051

MONTGOMERY WARD & COMPANY
619 West Chicago Avenue
Chicago, IL 60671
Principal Business: Diversified retailing
Contact: Personnel Department
Telephone: (312) 467-2000

MOORE BUSINESS FORMS, INC.
275 North Field Drive
Lake Forest, IL 60045
Principal Business: Manufacturing and marketing of business systems and forms
Contact: Director of Human Resources
Telephone: (708) 615-6000

J. P. MORGAN & COMPANY, INC.
60 Wall Street
New York, NY 10260
Principal Business: Financial services
Contact: Vice-President of Personnel
Telephone: (212) 648-3129

MOTOROLA, INC.
4250 East Camelback Road
Phoenix, AZ 85018
Principal Business: Manufacturing and marketing of electronic systems and components
Contact: Coordinator of College Recruitment
Telephone: (708) 538-2364

NABISCO BISCUIT COMPANY
100 DeForest Avenue
East Hanover, NJ 07936
Principal Business: Manufacturing and marketing of food products
Contact: Manager of Professional Recruiting
Telephone: (201) 503-2000

NATIONAL CAR RENTAL SYSTEM, INC.
7700 France Avenue South

Minneapolis, MN 55435
  Principal Business: Vehicle rental
  services
  Contact: Director of Human Resources
  Telephone: (612) 893-6060
NATIONAL CITY CORPORATION
1900 East Ninth Street
Cleveland, OH 44114
  Principal Business: Financial
  services
  Contact: Vice-President of College
  Relations
NATIONAL STEEL CORPORATION
20 Stanwix Street
Pittsburgh, PA 15222
  Principal Business: Manufacturing and
  marketing of steel products
  Contact: Coordinator of Employment
  and Personnel Services
  Telephone: (412) 394-6876
NATIONAL WESTMINSTER BANK
175 Water Street
New York, NY 10038
  Principal Business: Financial
  services
  Contact: Manager of College
  Recruiting
  Telephone: (212) 602-1645
NATIONWIDE INSURANCE COMPANY
One Nationwide Plaza
Columbus, OH 43216
  Principal Business: Insurance and
  other financial services
  Contact: Management Counselor
  Telephone: (614) 249-6561
**NAVISTAR INTERNATIONAL TRANSPORTATION
CORPORATION**
455 North CityFront Plaza Drive
Chicago, IL 60611
  Principal Business: Manufacturing and
  marketing of commercial vehicles
  Contact: Personnel Administration
  Telephone: (312) 836-3241
NCNB CORPORATION
One NCNB Plaza
Charlotte, NC 28255
  Principal Business: Financial
  services
  Contact: Manager of College
  Recruiting
  Telephone: (704) 374-8235

NCR CORPORATION
World Headquarters
1700 South Patterson Boulevard
Dayton, OH 45479
  Principal Business: Manufacturing
  and marketing of computers and
  information systems
  Contact: Director of Recruitment &
  College Relations
  Telephone: (513) 445-2342
NEC AMERICA, INC.
14040 Park Center Road
Herndon, VA 22071
  Principal Business: Manufacturing
  and marketing of high-technology
  equipment
  Contact: Corporate College
  Recruitment Officer
  Telephone: (703) 834-4000
NEIMAN-MARCUS
Main & Ervay Streets
Dallas, TX 75201
  Principal Business: Specialty store
  retailing
  Contact: Vice-President of Executive
  Personnel
  Telephone: (214) 573-5688
NESTLE USA, INC.
800 North Brand Boulevard
Glendale, CA 91203
  Principal Business: Manufacturing and
  marketing of food products
  Contact: Manager of College Relations
  & Recruitment
  Telephone: (818) 549-6000
NEW ENGLAND TELEPHONE
125 South Street
Boston, MA 02110
  Principal Business: Telecommunica-
  tions services and equipment
  Contact: Director of
  Employment
  Telephone: (617) 743-4201
NEW YORK LIFE INSURANCE COMPANY
51 Madison Avenue
New York, NY 10010
  Principal Business: Insurance and
  other financial services
  Contact: Assistant Vice-President,
  Employment Division
  Telephone: (212) 576-6702

NEW YORK TELEPHONE
1095 Avenue of the Americas
New York, NY 10036
  Principal Business: Telecommunica-
  tions services and equipment
  Contact: Management
  Employment
  Telephone: (212) 395-7097

NFO RESEARCH, INC.
2 Pickwick Plaza
Greenwich, CT 06830
  Principal Business: Marketing
  research and information services
  Contact: Placement Department
  Telephone: (203) 629-8888

NIELSEN MARKETING RESEARCH
Nielsen Plaza
Northbrook, IL 60062
  Principal Business: Marketing
  research and information services
  Contact: Regional Human Resources
  Manager
  Telephone: (708) 205-4247

NIKE, INC.
1 Bowerman Drive
Beaverton, OR 97005
  Principal Business: Manufacturing and
  marketing of footwear and apparel
  products
  Contact: Personnel Department
  Telephone: (503) 671-6453

NORDSON CORPORATION
28601 Clemens Road
Westlake, OH 44145
  Principal Business: Manufacturing and
  marketing of industrial application
  equipment and related computer
  software
  Contact: Manager of Organizational
  Development and Corporate Human
  Resources

NORTHERN TELECOM, INC.
Northern Telecom Plaza
200 Athens Way
Nashville, TN 37228
  Principal Business: Manufacturing
  and marketing of telecommunications
  equipment and network systems
  Contact: Manager, Staffing and
  College Relations
  Telephone: (615) 734-4625

NORTHWEST AIRLINES, INC.
Minneapolis/St. Paul International
Airport
MS A1470
St. Paul, MN 55111
  Principal Business: Air
  Transportation
  Contact: Director of Human Resources
  Telephone: (612) 726-2214

**NORTHWESTERN MUTUAL LIFE INSURANCE
COMPANY**
720 East Wisconsin Avenue
Milwaukee, WI 53202
  Principal Business: Insurance and
  other financial services
  Contact: Assistant Director for
  Manpower Development
  Telephone: (414) 299-1677

NORTON COMPANY
One New Bond Street
Worcester, MA 01615
  Principal Business: Manufacturing
  and marketing of abrasives and
  engineering materials
  Contact: Supervisor of Personnel
  Telephone: (508) 795-2931

NUTRI/SYSTEM, INC.
380 Sentry Parkway
Blue Bell, PA 19422
  Principal Business: Weight-loss
  services and food products
  Contact: College Recruitment
  Coordinator
  Telephone: (800) 777-7892

OGILVY & MATHER WORLDWIDE, INC.
Worldwide Plaza
309 West 49th Street
New York, NY 10019
  Principal Business: Advertising
  services
  Contact: Personnel Department
  Telephone: (212) 237-4000

OHIO BELL TELEPHONE COMPANY
45 Erieview Plaza
Cleveland, OH 44114
  Principal Business: Telecommunica-
  tions services and equipment
  Contact: Coordinator of Professional
  Employment
  Telephone: (216) 384-4559

OHIO EDISON COMPANY

76 South Main Street
Akron, OH 44308
  Principal Business: Electrical
  utility services
  Contact: Coordinator of Professional
  Employment

OTIS ELEVATOR
Ten Farm Springs
Farmington, CT 06032
  Principal Business: Manufacturing and
  marketing of elevators and escalators
  Contact: Manager of Corporate
  Staffing

OWENS-CORNING FIBERGLAS CORPORATION
Fiberglas Tower
Toledo, OH 43659
  Principal Business: Manufacturing
  and marketing of building and
  construction materials
  Contact: Employment Specialist
  Telephone: (419) 248-6874

OWENS-LLINOIS, INC.
One SeaGate
Toledo, OH 43666
  Principal Business: Manufacturing and
  marketing of glass, plastics, and
  metal packaging
  Contact: Director of Human Resources
  Telephone: (419) 247-1855

OXFORD INDUSTRIES, INC.
P.O. Box 54600
Atlanta, GA 30308
  Principal Business: Manufacturing and
  marketing of apparel
  Contact: Manager of Employment &
  Training
  Telephone: (404) 653-1351

PACKAGING CORPORATION OF AMERICA
1603 Orrington Avenue
Evanston, IL 60204
  Principal Business: Manufacturing and
  marketing of containers
  Contact: Director of Human Resources
  Telephone: (708) 492-5745

PALL CORPORATION
2200 Northern Boulevard
East Hills, NY 11548
  Principal Business: Manufacturing and
  marketing of filtration systems
  Contact: Corporate Employment Manager
  Telephone: (516) 484-5400

PARAMOUNT COMMUNICATIONS
15 Columbus Circle
New York, NY 10023
  Principal Business: Entertainment
  services
  Contact: Personnel Department
  Telephone: (212) 373-8000

PARISIAN, INC.
750 Lakeshore Parkway
Birmingham, AL 35211
  Principal Business: Apparel Retailing
  Contact: Manager of Merchant
  Placement and Development
  Telephone: (205) 940-4127

PARKE-DAVIS
201 Tabor Road
Morris Plains, NJ 07950
  Principal Business: Manufacturing and
  marketing of pharmaceutical products
  Contact: Director of Human Resources,
  Sales & Marketing
  Telephone: (800) 722-4783

PARKER HANNIFIN CORPORATION
17325 Euclid Avenue
Cleveland, OH 44112
  Principal Business: Manufacturing
  and marketing of motion-control
  components and systems
  Contact: Manager of Human Resource
  Development
  Telephone: (216) 531-3000, Extension
  2384

PAYLESS DRUG STORES
9275 Southwest Peyton Lane
Wilsonville, OR 97070
  Principal Business: Drugstore
  retailing
  Contact: Recruiting Coordinator
  Telephone: (503) 682-4100

PAYLESS SHOESOURCE
P.O. Box 1189
Topeka, KS 66601
  Principal Business: Footwear
  retailing
  Contact: Manager of College Relations
  Telephone: (913) 233-5171, Extension
  2011

J. C. PENNEY COMPANY, INC.
P.O. Box 659000
Dallas, TX 75265
  Principal Business: Department store

retailing
Contact: College Relations Manager
Telephone: (214) 591-2316

PENNZOIL COMPANY
P.O. Box 2967
Houston, TX 77252
Principal Business: Petroleum and gas
refining and marketing
Contact: Senior Human Resources
Representative
Telephone: (713) 546-4483

PEPSI-COLA
Six North, MD #602
Routes 35 & 100
Somers, NY 10589
Principal Business: Manufacturing and
marketing of soft drinks
Contact: Campus Recruiting Manager
Telephone: (914) 767-7479

PET INCORPORATED
P.O. Box 392
St. Louis, MO 63166
Principal Business: Manufacturing
and marketing of specialty foods and
confections
Contact: Manager of Recruiting

PFIZER, INC.
235 East 42nd Street
New York, NY 10017
Principal Business: Manufacturing
and marketing of health-care
and other products
Contact: University Relations
Coordinator
Telephone: (212) 573-2236

PHILIP MORRIS COMPANIES, INC.
120 Park Avenue
New York, NY 10017
Principal Business: Manufacturing and
marketing of tobacco, beer, and food
products
Contact: Specialist in College
Relations
Telephone: (212) 878-2098

PHILLIPS PETROLEUM COMPANY
180 Plaza Building
Bartlesville, OK 74004
Principal Business: Petroleum
refining and marketing
Contact: Director of Employment &
Placement

Telephone: (918) 661-5630

PILLSBURY BRANDS
200 South Sixth Street
MS 38R5
Minneapolis, MN 55402
Principal Business: Manufacturing and
marketing of food products
Contact: College Recruiting
Coordinator
Telephone: (612) 330-5154

PITNEY BOWES, INC.
Walter H. Wheeler, Jr. Drive
Stamford, CT 06926
Principal Business: Manufacturing and
marketing of business equipment
Contact: Manager of College Relations
Telephone: (203) 351-7447

PIZZA HUT, INC.
9111 East Douglas
Wichita, KS 67207
Principal Business: Fast-food
franchising
Contact: Human Resource Development,
College Relations
Telephone: (316) 681-9000

PLAYTEX FAMILY PRODUCTS CORPORATION
700 Fairfield Avenue
Stamford, CT 06904
Principal Business: Manufacturing and
marketing of personal-care products
Contact: Corporate Recruiting

POLAROID CORPORATION
575 Technology Square
Cambridge, MA 02139
Principal Business: Manufacturing and
marketing of cameras, photographic
films, and related devices
Contact: College Relations Manager
Telephone: (617) 577-4354

PREMIER INDUSTRIAL CORPORATION
4500 Euclid Avenue
Cleveland, OH 44103
Principal Business: Marketing of
industrial products and components
Contact: Corporate Director of
Recruiting
Telephone: (216) 391-8300

PRENTICE-HALL
113 Sylvan Avenue
Englewood Cliffs, NJ 07632
Principal Business: Publishing and

marketing of college textbooks
Contact: Director of Sales
Telephone: (201) 592-2210

PRESTO PRODUCTS
P.O. Box 2399
Appleton, WI 54913
Principal Business: Manufacturing and
marketing of plastic wrap, bags, and
containers
Contact: Employment Manager
Telephone: (414) 739-9471

PROCTER & GAMBLE
Two P&G Plaza
Cincinnati, OH 45202
Principal Business: Manufacturing
and marketing of household, personal-
care, food, and other products
Contact: Manager of U.S. Corporate
Recruiting
Telephone: (513) 983-3788

PROMUS COMPANIES
1023 Cherry Road
Memphis, TN 38117
Principal Business: Hotel and casino
services
Contact: Supervisor of College
Relations
Telephone: (901) 762-8832

PRUDENTIAL INSURANCE COMPANY OF AMERICA
56 North Livingston Avenue
Roseland, NJ 07068
Principal Business: Insurance and
other financial services
Contact: Corporate Employment Center
Telephone: (201) 716-2386

QUAKER OATS COMPANY
321 North Clark Street
Chicago, IL 60604
Principal Business: Manufacturing
and marketing of food and beverage
products
Contact: Manager of College
Recruiting
Telephone: (312) 222-8843

QUOTRON SYSTEMS, INC.
12731 West Jefferson Boulevard
Los Angeles, CA 90066
Principal Business: Financial
information services
Contact: Human Resources Manager
Telephone: (213) 302-4072

RADIO SHACK
200 West 22nd Street
Lombard, IL 60148
Principal Business: Electronics
retailing
Contact: Employment Manager
Telephone: (708) 916-7060

RALSTON PURINA COMPANY
Checkerboard Square
St. Louis, MO 63164
Principal Business: Manufacturing and
marketing of food products
Contact: Manager of College Relations
Telephone: (319) 323-3353

RAYCHEM CORPORATION
MS 111/8202
300 Constitution Drive
Menlo Park, CA 94025
Principal Business: Manufacturing
and marketing of advanced technology
components and systems
Contact: Manager of College Relations
Telephone: (415) 361-7758

RAYMOND CORPORATION
Canal Street
Greene, NY 13778
Principal Business: Manufacturing
and marketing of forklift trucks and
materials-handling systems
Contact: Staffing Manager

RAYTHEON COMPANY
141 Spring Street
Lexington, MA 02173
Principal Business: Diversified
manufacturing and services
Contact: Manager of College Programs
Telephone: (617) 860-2565

REEBOK INTERNATIONAL
100 Technology Center Drive
Stoughton, A 02072
Principal Business: Manufacturing and
marketing of footwear and apparel
products
Contact: Personnel Department
Telephone: (617) 341-5000

REED TOOL COMPANY
6501 Navigation Boulevard
Houston, TX 77011
Principal Business: Manufacturing and
marketing of drill bits
Contact: Manager of Labor Relations

Telephone: (713) 924-5200
REVLON, INC.
625 Madison Avenue
New York, NY 10022
  Principal Business: Manufacturing and
  marketing of personal-care products
  Contact: Personnel Department
  Telephone: (212) 527-4000
REYNOLDS METALS COMPANY
6601 West Broad Street
Richmond, VA 23230
  Principal Business: Manufacturing and
  marketing of aluminum products
  Contact: Director of Employment &
  Placement
  Telephone: (804) 281-4847
RJR NABISCO
1301 Avenue of the Americas
New York, NY 10019
  Principal Business: Manufacturing
  and marketing of food and tobacco
  products
  Contact: Personnel Department
  Telephone: (212) 258-5600
ROBINSON'S DEPARTMENT STORES
600 West Seventh Street
Los Angeles, CA 90017
  Principal Business: Department store
  retailing
  Contact: Manager of Executive
  Placement
  Telephone: (213) 488-7895
ROCHESTER INSTRUMENT SYSTEMS, INC.
255 North Union Street
Rochester, NY 14605
  Principal Business: Manufacturing and
  marketing of electronic instrument
  controls
  Contact: Personnel Supervisor
  Telephone: (716) 263-7700, Extension
  4983
ROHM AND HAAS COMPANY
Independence Mall West
Philadelphia, PA 19105
  Principal Business: Manufacturing and
  marketing of specialty chemicals
  Contact: Manager of Corporate
  Staffing
  Telephone: (215) 592-6967
RUBBERMAID, INC.
1147 Akron Road

Wooster, OH 44691
  Principal Business: Manufacturing
  and marketing of plastic and rubber
  consumer goods
  Contact: Salaried Human Resources
  Telephone: (216) 262-6000
RYDER SYSTEM, INC.
3600 Northwest 82nd Avenue
Miami, FL 33166
  Principal Business: Vehicle rental
  services
  Contact: Corporate Manager of Human
  Resources
  Telephone: (305) 593-4049
SAATCHI & SAATCHI, INC.
375 Hudson Street
New York, NY 10014
  Principal Business: Advertising
  services
  Contact: Personnel Department
  Telephone: (212) 463-2000
SAFECO CORPORATION
Safeco Plaza
Seattle, WA 98185
  Principal Business: Insurance and
  other financial services
  Contact: Employment Center
SAINT PAUL COMPANIES
385 Washington Street
St. Paul, MN 55102
  Principal Business: Insurance and
  other financial services
  Contact: College Relations Manager
  Telephone: (612) 228-5839
SAKS FIFTH AVENUE
611 Fifth Avenue
New York, NY 10022
  Principal Business: Specialty store
  retailing
  Contact: Manager of College Relations
  Telephone: (212) 940-4788
SAMSONITE CORPORATION
11200 East 45th Avenue
Denver, CO 80239
  Principal Business: Manufacturing
  and marketing of luggage and business
  cases
  Contact: Vice-President of Human
  Resources
  Telephone: (303) 373-7468
SARA LEE HOSIERY

P.O. Box 2495
Winston-Salem, NC 27102
  Principal Business: Manufacturing and
  marketing of hosiery
  Contact: Employment Manager
  Telephone: (919) 744-8624

SARA LEE KNIT PRODUCTS
P.O. Box 3019
Winston-Salem, NC 27102
  Principal Business: Manufacturing and
  marketing of undergarments
  Contact: Management Recruiter
  Telephone: (919) 744-2166

SCHERING-PLOUGH CORPORATION
60 Orange Street
Bloomfield, NJ 07003
  Principal Business: Manufacturing
  and marketing of pharmaceutical and
  consumer products
  Contact: Director of Personnel
  Operations

SEAFIRST CORPORATION
P.O. Box 3977
Seattle, WA 98124
  Principal Business: Financial
  services
  Contact: College Relations
  Telephone: (206) 358-7508

SEARS, ROEBUCK & COMPANY
Sears Tower
Chicago, IL 60684
  Principal Business: Department store
  and catalog retailing
  Contact: Manager of College
  Recruiting
  Telephone: (312) 875-4200

SENTRY INSURANCE
1800 North Point Drive
Stevens Point, WI 54481
  Principal Business: Insurance
  services
  Contact: Director of Human Resources

SERVICE MASTER COMPANY
2300 Warrenville Road
Downers Grove, IL 60515
  Principal Business: Cleaning, lawn
  care, and pest control services
  Contact: Vice-President for People
  Telephone: (312) 964-1300

SERVICE MERCHANDISE COMPANY, INC.
P.O. Box 24600

Nashville, TN 37202
  Principal Business: Catalog showroom
  retailing
  Contact: Manager of Human Resources
  Telephone: (615) 660-4620

SEWELL PLASTICS, INC.
P.O. Box 43325
Atlanta, GA 30336
  Principal Business: Manufacturing and
  marketing of plastic containers
  Contact: Employment & Employee
  Services Manager
  Telephone: (404) 691-4256

SHAW INDUSTRIES
616 Walnut Avenue
MD 068-15
P.O. Box 2128
Dalton, GA 30722
  Principal Business: Manufacturing and
  marketing of carpeting
  Contact: Manager of College
  Recruiting
  Telephone: (404) 275-2370

SHELL OIL COMPANY
P.O. Box 2463
Houston, TX 77252
  Principal Business: Petroleum
  refining and marketing
  Contact: Manager of Recruitment
  Telephone: (713) 241-4278

SHERWIN-WILLIAMS COMPANY
101 Prospect Avenue, Northwest
Cleveland, OH 44115
  Principal Business: Manufacturing and
  marketing of paint and paint store
  retailing
  Contact: Employment Administrator
  Telephone: (216) 566-2074

SHOPKO STORES, INC.
700 Pilgrim Way
P.O. Box 19060-9060
Green Bay, WI 54307
  Principal Business: Food store
  retailing
  Contact: Manager of Executive
  Recruiting
  Telephone: (414) 496-4185

SIECOR CORPORATION
489 Siecor Park
Hickory, NC 28603
  Principal Business: Manufacturing and

marketing of cable and ancillary equipment for the telecommunications and other industries
Contact: Campus Relations
Telephone: (704) 327-5213

SIGNET BANKING CORPORATION
P.O. Box 25970
Richmond, VA 23260
Principal Business: Financial services
Contact: Manager of College Relations
Telephone: (804) 771-7565

SIZZLER INTERNATIONAL, INC.
12655 West Jefferson Boulevard
Los Angeles, CA 90066
Principal Business: Restaurant retailing
Contact: Management Selection Associate
Telephone: (213) 827-2300

SKY CHEFS
P.O. Box 61977
Dallas/Forth Worth Airport
TX 75261
Principal Business: Food services
Contact: Senior Personnel Representative
Telephone: (817) 792-2473

SMITH CORONA CORPORATION
P.O. Box 2020
Cortland, NY 13045
Principal Business: Manufacturing and marketing of electronic typewriters, word processors, and personal computers
Contact: Manager of Personnel
Telephone: (607) 753-6011

SMITHKLINE BEECHAM
P.O. Box 1539
King of Prussia, PA 19406
Principal Business: Manufacturing and marketing of pharmaceutical and consumer products
Contact: Employment Manager
Telephone: (215) 270-6397

J. M. SMUCKER COMPANY
Strawberry Lane
Orrville, OH 44667
Principal Business: Manufacturing and marketing of jams, jellies, and other food products

Contact: Corporate Recruiter
Telephone: (216) 682-3000, Extension 3510

SNAP-ON TOOLS CORPORATION
2801 80th Street
Kenosha, WI 53141
Principal Business: Manufacturing and marketing of automotive tools and related equipment
Contact: Senior Personnel Representative
Telephone: (414) 656-5586

SONOCO PRODUCTS COMPANY
P.O. Box 160
Hartsville, SC 29550
Principal Business: Manufacturing and marketing of packaging products
Contact: Corporate Employment Manager
Telephone: (803) 383-7764

SONY CORPORATION OF AMERICA
Sony Drive
Park Ridge, NJ 07656
Principal Business: Manufacturing and marketing of electronic equipment
Contact: Manager of University Relations
Telephone: (201) 930-7353

SOUTHERN NEW ENGLAND TELECOMMUNICATIONS COMPANY
367 Orange Street
New Haven, CT 06511
Principal Business: Telecommunications services and equipment
Contact: Director of Management Employment
Telephone: (203) 771-3530

SOUTHWESTERN BELL CORPORATION
One Bell Center
Suite 3600
St. Louis, MO 63101
Principal Business: Telecommunications services and equipment
Contact: Director of College Recruiting
Telephone: (314) 235-5494

SOUTHWESTERN BELL TELEPHONE COMPANY
220 East Sixth Street
Topeka, KS 66603
Principal Business: Telecommunications services and equipment
Contact: District Manager of Employment & EEO

SPANG & COMPANY
P.O. Box 751
Butler, PA 16003
  Principal Business: Manufacturing and
  marketing of electronic components,
  transformers, metals, and toys
  Contact: Director of Personnel
  Telephone: (412) 287-8781, Extension
  5290

SPENCER GIFTS, INC.
1050 Black Horse Park
Pleasantville, NJ 08232
  Principal Business: Specialty store
  retailing
  Contact: Vice-President of Human
  Resources
  Telephone: (609) 645-3300

SPRINGS INDUSTRIES, INC.
205 North White Street
Fort Mill, SC 29715
  Principal Business: Manufacturing and
  marketing of textile products
  Contact: Director of Development and
  Administrative Personnel
  Telephone: (803) 547-3761

SQUARE D COMPANY
1415 South Roselle Road
Palatine, IL 60067
  Principal Business: Manufacturing
  and marketing of heavy equipment,
  industrial controls, transformers,
  and other products
  Contact: Corporate Manager for
  Professional Employment
  Telephone: (708) 397-2600

SRI INTERNATIONAL
333 Ravenswood Avenue
Menlo Park, CA 94025
  Principal Business: Marketing
  research and information services
  Contact: Manager of Group Human
  Resources
  Telephone: (415) 859-5748

STACKPOLE CARBON COMPANY
201 Stackpole Street
St. Marys, PA 15857
  Principal Business: Manufacturing and
  marketing of carbon-based products
  Contact: Vice-President of Human
  Resources
  Telephone: (814) 781-1234

STAPLES
P.O. Box 9328
Framingham, MA 01701
  Principal Business: Office supply and
  equipment stores
  Contact: Corporate Recruiter
  Telephone: (508) 370-8637

STATE FARM INSURANCE COMPANIES
One State Farm Plaza
Bloomington, IL 61710
  Principal Business: Insurance
  services
  Contact: Assistant Director of
  Personnel Relations
  Telephone: (309) 766-2664

STEELCASE, INC.
P.O. Box 1967
Grand Rapids, MI 49501
  Principal Business: Manufacturing and
  marketing of office furniture
  Contact: Employment Representative
  for College Relations
  Telephone: (616) 247-3208

STERLING, INC.
375 Ghent Road
Akron, OH 44333
  Principal Business: Jewelry store
  retailing
  Contact: Corporate Recruitment
  Manager
  Telephone: (216) 668-5000

STERLING WINTHROP, INC.
90 Park Avenue
New York, NY 10016
  Principal Business: Manufacturing and
  marketing of pharmaceutical and other
  health-care products
  Contact: Executive Employment
  Specialist
  Telephone: (212) 907-3359

STERNS
Route Four
Bergen Mall
Paramus, NJ 07652
  Principal Business: Department store
  retailing
  Contact: Director of Executive
  Placement
  Telephone: (201) 845-2426

STOUFFER FOODS CORPORATION
5750 Harper Road

Solon, OH 44139
  Principal Business: Manufacturing and
  marketing of food products
  Contact: Director of Human Resource
  Services
  Telephone: (216) 248-3600
STRAWBRIDGE & CLOTHIER
801 Market Street
Philadelphia, PA 19107
  Principal Business: Department store
  retailing
  Contact: Manager of Executive
  Recruitment and Placement
  Telephone: (215) 629-7817
SUN BANKS, INC.
200 South Orange Avenue
Orlando, FL 32801
  Principal Business: Financial
  services
  Contact: Training Manager
  Telephone: (407) 237-4336
SUN MICROSYSTEMS, INC.
2550 Garcia Avenue
M/S PAL1-408
Mountain View, CA 94043
  Principal; Business: Manufacturing
  and marketing of computer work-
  stations
  Contact: Manager of University
  Relations
  Telephone: (415) 336-0475
SUNBEAM
1621 Highway 15 North
Laurel, MS 39441
  Principal Business: Manufacturing and
  marketing of automatic blankets and
  small appliances
  Contact: Director of Human Resources
  Telephone: (601) 649-6170, Extension
317
SUPER VALU STORES, INC.
P.O. Box 990
Minneapolis, MN 55440
  Principal Business: Food wholesaling
  and retailing
  Contact: Human Resources Counselor
  Telephone: (612) 828-4653
TACO BELL CORPORATION
17901 Von Karman Avenue
Irvine, CA 92714
  Principal Business: Fast-food

franchising
  Contact: Manager of National
  Recruiting Programs
  Telephone: (714) 863-5284
TAMBRANDS
777 Westchester Avenue
White Plains, NY 10604
  Principal Business: Manufacturing and
  marketing of personal-care products
  Contact: Director of Compensation and
  Benefits
  Telephone: (914) 696-6000
TANDY CORPORATION
500 One Tandy Center
Forth Worth, TX 76102
  Principal Business: Manufacturing and
  retailing (through Radio Shack) of
  electronics products
  Contact: Regional Employment Manager
  Telephone: (817) 878-6893
TARGET STORES
33 South Sixth Street
Minneapolis, MN 55440
  Principal Business: Discount
  department-store retailing
  Contact: Senior College Relations
  Representative
TEKTRONIX, INC.
50-480, P.O. Box 50
Beaverton, OR 97077
  Principal Business: Manufacturing and
  marketing of measurement instruments
  Contact: Manager of Corporate
  Staffing
  Telephone: (503) 627-6974
TENNECO, INC.
P.O. Box 2511
Houston, TX 77252
  Principal Business: Manufacturing and
  marketing of natural gas, machinery,
  ship-building, and other products
  Contact: Human Resources Supervisor
  Telephone: (713) 757-4002
TEXACO, INC.
P.O. Box 1404
Houston, TX 77251
  Principal Business: Petroleum
  refining and marketing
  Contact: Manager of Professional
  Employment
  Telephone: (713) 752-7954

TEXAS INSTRUMENTS, INC.
MS 3951
P.O. Box 650311
Dallas, TX 75265
  Principal Business: Manufacturing and
  marketing of semiconductor materials,
  electronics, and computers
  Contact: Manager of Corporate
  University Relations
  Telephone: (214) 917-4566

TEXTRON, INC.
25200 West Rye Canyon Road
Valencia, CA 91355
  Principal Business: Manufacturing and
  marketing of fluid and electronic
  control systems and components, and
  flight-control systems and components
  Contact: Manager of Professional
  Employment
  Telephone: (805) 253-5845

THILMANY COMPANY
P.O. Box 600
Kaukauna, WI 54130
  Principal Business: Manufacturing
  and marketing of paper and forest
  products
  Contact: Personnel Analyst
  Telephone: (414) 766-4611

J. WALTER THOMPSON COMPANY
466 Lexington Avenue
New York, NY 10017
  Principal Business: Advertising
  services
  Contact: Personnel Department
  Telephone: (212) 210-7000

3M
3M Center
224-1W-02
St. Paul, MN 55144
  Principal Business: Diversified
  manufacturing and services
  Contact: Manager of College Relations
  Telephone: (612) 733-1755

TIME, INC.
1271 Avenue of the Americas
New York, NY 10020
  Principal Business: Communications
  products and services
  Contact: Manager of College Relations
  Telephone: (212) 841-2260

TIME WARNER

75 Rockefeller Plaza
New York, NY 10019
  Principal Business: Communications
  products and services
  Contact: Personnel Department
  Telephone: (212) 484-8000

TORRINGTON COMPANY
59 Field Street
Torrington, CT 06790
  Principal Business: Manufacturing and
  marketing of needle, roller, and ball
  bearings
  Contact: Manager of Professional
  Recruiting
  Telephone: (203) 482-9512

TOYS "R" US
461 From Road
Paramus, NJ 07652
  Principal Business: Toy and clothing
  store retailing
  Contact: Manager of Human Resource
  Planning
  Telephone: (201) 599-7901

TRAVELERS COMPANIES
One Tower Square
1-30 CR
Hartford, CT 06183
  Principal Business: Insurance and
  other financial services
  Contact: Assistant Director of
  College Relations
  Telephone: (203) 954-8113

TREMCO, INC.
3735 Green Road
Beachwood, OH 44122
  Principal Business: Manufacturing
  and marketing of caulking and
  waterproofing products
  Contact: Human Resources Manager
  Telephone: (216) 292-5000

TRW, INC.
1900 Richmond Road
Cleveland, OH 44124
  Principal Business: Diversified
  manufacturing and services
  Contact: Director of University
  Relations and Associates Program
  Telephone: (216) 291-7416

TYSON FOODS, INC.
P.O. Drawer 2020
Springdale, AR 72765

Principal Business: Manufacturing and marketing of food products
Contact: Manager of Recruitment and Management Development
Telephone: (501) 756-4000

UNILEVER UNITED STATES, INC.
390 Park Avenue
New York, NY 10022
Principal Business: Manufacturing and marketing of food and personal-care products
Contact: Director of MBA Recruiting
Telephone: (212) 906-3583

UNION CARBIDE CORPORATION
39 Old Ridgebury Road
Danbury, CT 06817
Principal Business: Manufacturing and marketing of chemicals, industrial gases, and other products
Contact: Manager of Professional Placement
Telephone: (203) 794-6516

UNIROYAL GOODRICH TIRE COMPANY
600 South Main Street
Akron, OH 44397
Principal Business: Manufacturing and marketing of tires
Contact: Manager of Employee Relations and Professional Staffing
Telephone: (216) 374-2177

UNITED AIRLINES
P.O. Box 66100
Chicago, IL 60666
Principal Business: Air transportation
Contact: Manager of College Relations
Telephone: (708) 952-5915

UNITED TECHNOLOGIES CORPORATION
One Financial Plaza
Hartford, CT 06101
Principal Business: Manufacturing and marketing of high-technology products
Contact: Manager of University Relations
Telephone: (203) 728-7631

UNITEK CORPORATION
2724 South Peck Road
Monrovia, CA 91016
Principal Business: Manufacturing and marketing of orthodontic and dental products and equipment

Contact: Employment

UNOCAL CORPORATION
P.O. Box 7600
Los Angeles, CA 90051
Principal Business: Petroleum and gas refining and marketing
Contact: Manager of Recruitment and College Relations
Telephone: (213) 977-7878

UPJOHN COMPANY
7000 Portage Road
Kalamazoo, MI 49001
Principal Business: Manufacturing and marketing of pharmaceutical and other health-care products
Contact: Personnel Department
Telephone: (616) 323-4000

USF&G CORPORATION
P.O. Box 1138
Baltimore, MD 21203
Principal Business: Insurance and other financial services
Contact: Human Resources Specialist
Telephone: (301) 234-2309

USG CORPORATION
101 South Wacker Drive
Chicago, IL 60606
Principal Business: Manufacturing and marketing of building materials
Contact: Manager of Human Resources Planning
Telephone: (312) 606-4000

U.S. SPRINT/UNITED TELECOM
P.O. Box 11315
Kansas City, MO 64112
Principal Business: Telecommunications services
Contact: Manager of University Relations

U.S. STEEL
600 Grant Street
Pittsburgh, PA 15219
Principal Business: Manufacturing and marketing of steel and other products
Contact: Manager of Human Resources
Telephone: (412) 433-6688

U.S. WEST
188 Inverness Drive West
Englewood, CO 80112
Principal Business: Telecommunications services and equipment

Contact: Director of Recruiting
Telephone: (303) 741-8454

UTICA NATIONAL INSURANCE GROUP
P.O. Box 530
Utica, NY 13503
  Principal Business: Insurance
  services
  Contact: Employment Coordinator
  Telephone: (315) 734-2292

VALLEY NATIONAL CORPORATION
B301
P.O. Box 71
Phoenix, AZ 85001
  Principal Business: Financial
  services
  Contact: Corporate Recruiter
  Telephone: (602) 221-4478

VAN DEN BERGH FOODS COMPANY
2200 Cabot Drive
Lisle, IL 60532
  Principal Business: Manufacturing and
  marketing of food products
  Contact: Director of Management
  Development
  Telephone: (708) 955-5480

VANITY FAIR MILLS
624 South Alabama Avenue
Monroeville, AL 36462
  Principal Business: Manufacturing and
  marketing of apparel
  Contact: Director of Human Resources
  Development
  Telephone: (205) 575-3231, Extension
  2318

VICKERS, INC.
P.O. Box 302
Troy, MI 48007
  Principal Business: Manufacturing and
  marketing of fluid power systems,
  pumps, motors, and valves
  Contact: Staff Personnel
  Representative

VISA U.S.A.
P.O. Box 8999
San Francisco, CA 94128
  Principal Business: Financial
  transaction services
  Contact: Recruitment Coordinator
  Telephone: (415) 570-3775

VITRO CORPORATION
14000 Georgia Avenue

Silver Spring, MD 20906
  Principal Business: Developing and
  marketing of computer software
  Contact: College Relations
  Coordinator
  Telephone: (301) 231-1147

WACHOVIA CORPORATION
P.O. Box 3099
Winston-Salem, NC 27150
  Principal Business: Financial
  services
  Contact: Vice-President of Recruiting
  and Placement
  Telephone: (919) 770-5209

WALGREEN COMPANY
200 Wilmot Road
Deerfield, IL 60015
  Principal Business: Drugstore
  retailing
  Contact: Corporate Manager for
  Recruitment
  Telephone: (708) 405-5888

WALKER GROUP
3939 Priority Way South Drive
Indianapolis, IN 46280
  Principal Business: Marketing
  research and information services
  Contact: Personnel Department
  Telephone: (317) 843-3939

WAL-MART STORES, INC.
People Division
702 Southwest Eighth
Bentonville, AR 72716
  Principal Business: Discount
  department stores and other retailing
  Contact: Director of College
  Relations
  Telephone: (501) 273-6559

WARNER BROS., INC.
4000 Warner Boulevard
Burbank, CA 91522
  Principal Business: Production and
  marketing of filmed entertainment
  Contact: Director of Recruitment
  Telephone: (818) 954-3150

WARNER-LAMBERT COMPANY
201 Tabor Road
Morris Plains, NJ 07950
  Principal Business: Manufacturing and
  marketing of health-care and consumer
  products

Contact: Manager of Corporate
Recruitment
Telephone: (201) 540-2000, Extension
2746

WAUSAU INSURANCE COMPANIES
2000 Westwood Drive
P.O. Box 8017
Wausau, WI 54402
Principal Business: Insurance
services
Contact: Human Resource Specialist
Telephone: (715) 842-6593

WELLS FARGO & COMPANY
394 Pacific Avenue
San Francisco, CA 94163
Principal Business: Financial
services
Contact: Manager of Recruitment and
Placement Services
Telephone: (415) 396-3846

WENDY'S INTERNATIONAL
P.O. Box 256
Dublin, OH 43017
Principal Business: Fast-food
franchising
Contact: Personnel Department
Telephone: (614) 764-3100

R. D. WERNER COMPANY, INC.
93 Werner Road
Greenville, PA 16125
Principal Business: Manufacturing and
marketing of ladders
Contact: Personnel Director
Telephone: (412) 588-8600, Extension
264

WEST POINT PEPPERELL, INC.
P.O. Box 71
West Point, GA 31833
Principal Business: Manufacturing and
marketing of textile products
Contact: Manager of Compensation and
Human Resources Administration
Telephone: (404) 645-4198

WESTINGHOUSE ELECTRIC CORPORATION
Westinghouse Building
Gateway Center
Pittsburgh, PA 15222
Principal Business: Diversified
manufacturing and services
Contact: Manager of Marketing
Development Program

Telephone: (412) 642-3357

WESTVACO CORPORATION
299 Park Avenue
New York, NY 10171
Principal Business: Manufacturing and
marketing of paper, packaging, and
specialty chemicals
Contact: Manager of College Relations
Telephone: (212) 688-5000, Extension
5294

WEYERHAEUSER COMPANY
QP-4
Tacoma, WA 98477
Principal Business: Manufacturing and
marketing of forest products
Contact: Manager of Recruiting and
Staffing Services
Telephone: (206) 924-6759

WHIRLPOOL CORPORATION
Administrative Center
2000 M-63 North
Benton Harbor, MI 49022
Principal Business: Manufacturing and
marketing of appliances
Contact: Director of Human Resource
Services
Telephone: (616) 926-5044

JOHN WILEY & SONS
605 Third Avenue
New York, NY 10158
Principal Business: Publishing and
marketing of books
Contact: Senior Employment/Employee
Relations Specialist
Telephone: (212) 850-6238

WILSON BRANDS
P.O. Box 26724
Oklahoma City, OK 73126
Principal Business: Manufacturing and
marketing of food products
Contact: Director of Human Resources

F.W. WOOLWORTH COMPANY
233 Broadway
New York, NY 10279
Principal Business: Variety and
specialty store retailing
Contact: Director of Human Resources
Telephone: (212) 553-2403

WRANGLER
P.O. Box 21488
Greensboro, NC 27420

Principal Business: Manufacturing and
marketing of apparel products
Contact: Coordinator of Employment
Telephone: (919) 373-4252

WM. WRIGLEY JR. COMPANY
410 North Michigan Avenue
Chicago, IL 60611
Principal Business: Manufacturing and
marketing of chewing gum
Contact: Personnel Department
Telephone: (312) 644-2121

XEROX CORPORATION
Xerox Square
Rochester, NY 14644
Principal Business: Manufacturing
and marketing of document-related
products
Contact: Manager of Corporate
Employment & College Relations
Telephone: (716) 423-3386

YELLOW FREIGHT SYSTEM, INC.
10990 Roe Avenue
Overland Park, KS 66211
Principal Business: Trucking services
Contact: Manager of Corporate
Employment
Telephone: (913) 345-3000

YORK INTERNATIONAL CORPORATION
Box 2202-36BB
York, PA 17405

Principal Business: Manufacturing
and marketing of air conditioning
and refrigeration equipment and
systems
Contact: Director of Labor Relations
and Human Resources
Telephone: (717) 771-7207

YOUNG & RUBICAM, INC.
285 Madison Avenue
New York, NY 10017
Principal Business: Advertising
services
Contact: Personnel Department
Telephone: (212) 210-3000

ZENITH DATA SYSTEMS
2150 East Lake Cook Road
Buffalo Grove, IL 60089
Principal Business: Manufacturing and
marketing of personal computers
Contact: Director of Human Resources
Telephone: (708) 808-4637

ZENITH ELECTRONICS CORPORATION
1000 Milwaukee Avenue
Glenview, IL 60025
Principal Business: Manufacturing and
marketing of televisions and related
products
Contact: Senior Personnel
Representative
Telephone: (708) 391-7162

CHAPTER FIVE

**PROFESSIONAL AND TRADE ASSOCIATIONS
IN MARKETING-RELATED FIELDS**

The names, addresses, and phone numbers of about 115 professional and trade associations are listed in this chapter. Two types of associations are listed: ones that specialize in functional areas of marketing (such as advertising, physical distribution, personal selling, retailing, marketing research, and public relations) and ones that focus on specific industries (such as banking, life insurance, dairy, frozen foods, and railroads).

If you have an interest in a particular area of marketing or a certain industry, it may be worthwhile for you to contact one or more of the associations cited in order to gain further information:

. Many of the associations publish booklets describing career opportunities, educational requirements, and starting salaries. These booklets are generally available either for free or at a nominal fee. Some associations also sponsor their own speakers' bureaus that make practicing experts available to come to your college or university to talk about careers in their specialties.

. The listing may assist you in developing a targeted mailing when you seek to obtain an internship, a part-time job in your field while attending college, and/or a full-time job at graduation.

. The listing may serve to encourage you to inquire as to how to join a relevant professional association. Several associations offer special reduced rates for student members. And, in addition to providing information on current developments in marketing, a number of associations offer reduced registration fees at seminars to students. These seminars may provide you with an important place to meet people in your intended career ("networking").

ADVERTISING COUNCIL
261 Madison Avenue
New York, NY 10016
(212) 922-1500
ADVERTISING RESEARCH FOUNDATION
3 East 54th Street
New York, NY 10022
(212) 751-5656
AMERICAN ADVERTISING FEDERATION
1400 K Street Northwest
Suite 1000
Washington, DC 20005
(202) 898-0089
AMERICAN ASSOCIATION FOR PUBLIC OPINION
RESEARCH
P.O. Box 17
Princeton, NJ 08542
(609) 924-8670
AMERICAN ASSOCIATION OF ADVERTISING
AGENCIES
666 Third Avenue
13th Floor
New York, NY 10017
(212) 682-2500
AMERICAN BANKERS ASSOCIATION
1120 Connecticut Avenue Northwest
Washington, DC 20036
(202) 663-5000
AMERICAN BOOKSELLERS ASSOCIATION
560 White Plains Road
Tarrytown, NY 10591
(914) 631-7800
AMERICAN COUNCIL OF LIFE INSURANCE
1001 Pennsylvania Avenue Northwest
Suite 500
Washington, DC 20004
(202) 624-2000
AMERICAN DAIRY ASSOCIATION
6300 North River Road
Rosemont, IL 60018
(708) 696-1880
AMERICAN FROZEN FOOD INSTITUTE
1764 Old Meadow Lane
Suite 350
McLean, VA 22102
(703) 821-0770
AMERICAN INSTITUTE OF FOOD DISTRIBUTION
28-12 Broadway
Fair Lawn, NJ 07410
(201) 791-5570
AMERICAN MARKETING ASSOCIATION

250 South Wacker Drive
Suite 200
Chicago, IL 60606
(312) 648-0536
AMERICAN PRODUCTION AND INVENTORY CONTROL
SOCIETY
500 West Annandale Road
Falls Church, VA 22046
(703) 237-8344
AMERICAN SOCIETY OF TRANSPORTATION AND
LOGISTICS
P.O. Box 33095
Louisville, KY 40232
(502) 451-8150
AMERICAN TELEMARKETING ASSOCIATION
5000 Van Nuys Boulevard
Number 300
Sherman Oaks, CA 91403
(818) 995-7338
AMERICAN TRUCKING ASSOCIATIONS
2200 Mill Road
Alexandria, VA 22314
(703) 838-1700
ASSOCIATION OF AMERICAN RAILROADS
Library Room 5800
50 F Street Northwest
Washington, DC 20001
(202) 639-2333
ASSOCIATION OF NATIONAL ADVERTISERS
155 East 44th Street
New York, NY 10017
(212) 697-5950
ASSOCIATION OF RETAIL MARKETING SERVICES
3 Caro Court
Red Bank, NJ 07701
(201) 842-5070
AUDIT BUREAU OF CIRCULATIONS
Communications Department
North Meacham Road
Schaumburg, IL 60173
(708) 605-0909
BANK MARKETING ASSOCIATION
309 West Washington Street
Chicago, IL 60606
(312) 782-1442
BIOMEDICAL MARKETING ASSOCIATION
310 North Alabama A100
Indianapolis, IN 46204
(317) 237-9100
BROADCAST PROMOTION AND MARKETING
EXECUTIVES

6255 Sunset Boulevard
Suite 624
Los Angeles, CA 90028
(213) 465-3777
BUREAU OF WHOLESALE SALES
REPRESENTATIVES (APPAREL)
1819 Peachtree Road Northeast
Suite 210
Atlanta, GA 30309
(404) 351-7355
BUSINESS/PROFESSIONAL ADVERTISING
ASSOCIATION
100 Metroplex Drive
Edison, NJ 08817
(908) 985-4441
BUSINESS PUBLICATIONS AUDIT OF
CIRCULATIONS
360 Park Avenue South
New York, NY 10010
(212) 532-6880
CHEMICAL MARKETING RESEARCH ASSOCIATION
60 Bay Street
Suite 702
Staten Island, NY 10301
(718) 876-8800
COLOR MARKETING GROUP
4001 North 9th Street
Suite 102
Arlington, VA 22203
(703) 528-7666
COUNCIL OF BETTER BUSINESS BUREAUS
4200 Wilson Boulevard
Suite 800
Arlington, VA 22203
(703) 276-0100
COUNCIL OF LOGISTICS MANAGEMENT
2803 Butterfield Road
Oak Brook, IL 60521
(312) 574-0985
COUNCIL OF SALES PROMOTION AGENCIES
750 Summer Street
Stamford, CT 06901
(203) 325-3911
DIRECT MARKETING ASSOCIATION
11 West 42nd Street
New York, NY 10036
(212) 768-7277
DIRECT MARKETING ASSOCIATION CATALOG
COUNCIL
11 West 42nd Street
New York, NY 10036

(212) 768-7277
DIRECT SELLING ASSOCIATION
1776 K Street Northwest
Suite 600
Washington, DC 20006
(202) 293-5760
EIGHT SHEET OUTDOOR ADVERTISING
ASSOCIATION
P.O. Box 39
Blue Springs, MO 64015
(816) 228-0900
ELECTRONIC MEDIA RATING COUNCIL
509 Madison Avenue
Suite 1112
New York, NY 10022
(212) 754-3343
FINANCIAL INSTITUTIONS MARKETING
ASSOCIATION
111 East Wacker Drive
Chicago, IL 60601
(312) 938-2570
FINANCIAL MARKETING ASSOCIATION
P.O. Box 14167
Madison, WI 53714
(608) 271-2664
FLORISTS' TRANSWORLD DELIVERY ASSOCIATION
29200 Northwestern Highway
Southfield, MI 48037
(313) 355-9300
FOOD MARKETING INSTITUTE
1750 K Street Northwest
Suite 700
Washington, DC 20006
(202) 452-8444
GROCERY MANUFACTURERS OF AMERICA
1010 Wisconsin Avenue Northwest
Suite 800
Washington, DC 20007
(202) 337-9400
HOBBY INDUSTRY ASSOCIATION OF AMERICA
319 East 54th Street
Elmwood Park, NJ 07407
(201) 794-1133
INCENTIVE MANUFACTURERS REPRESENTATIVES
ASSOCIATION
1555 Naperville/Wheaton Road
Suite 103B
Naperville, IL 60563
(708) 369-3466
INDEPENDENT INSURANCE AGENTS OF AMERICA
127 South Peyton

Alexandria, VA 22314
(703) 683-4422
INDUSTRIAL DESIGNERS SOCIETY OF AMERICA
1142 East Walker Road
Great Falls, VA 22066
(703) 759-0100
INDUSTRIAL DISTRIBUTION ASSOCIATION
3 Corporate Square
Suite 201
Atlanta, GA 30329
(404) 325-2776
INSTITUTE OF STORE PLANNERS
25 North Broadway
Tarrytown, NY 10591
(914) 332-1806
INSURANCE INFORMATION INSTITUTE
110 William Street
New York, NY 10038
(212) 669-9200
INTERNATIONAL ADVERTISING ASSOCIATION
342 Madison Avenue
20th Floor
Suite 2000
New York, NY 10017
(212) 557-1133
INTERNATIONAL ASSOCIATION OF BUSINESS
FORECASTING
Loyola College
Jenkins Hall, Room 211
4501 North Charles Street
Baltimore, MD 21210
(410) 323-1010
INTERNATIONAL COUNCIL OF SHOPPING CENTERS
665 Fifth Avenue
New York, NY 10022
(212) 421-8181
INTERNATIONAL FEDERATION OF ADVERTISING
AGENCIES
1450 East American Lane
Suite 1400
Schaumburg, IL 60173
(708) 330-6344
INTERNATIONAL FRANCHISE ASSOCIATION
1350 New York Avenue Northwest
Suite 900
Washington, DC 20005
(202) 628-8000
INTERNATIONAL MARKETING INSTITUTE
314 Hammond Street
Suite 52
Chestnut Hill, MA 02167

(617) 552-8690
INTERNATIONAL MASS RETAIL ASSOCIATION
1901 Pennsylvania Avenue Northwest
10th Floor
Washington, DC 20006
(202) 861-0774
INTERNATIONAL NEWSPAPER ADVERTISING AND
MARKETING EXECUTIVES
P.O. Box 17210
Washington, DC 20041
(703) 648-1168
INTERNATIONAL TRADE CLUB OF CHICAGO
203 North Wabash Avenue
Suite 1102
Chicago, IL 60601
(312) 368-9197
INTERNATIONAL TRADE COUNCIL
3144 Circle Hill Road
Alexandria, VA 22305
(703) 548-1234
JEWELERS OF AMERICA
1185 6th Avenue
30th Floor
New York, NY 10036
(212) 768-8777
LEAGUE OF ADVERTISING AGENCIES
2 South End Avenue
Number 4-C
New York, NY 10280
(212) 945-4314
MANUFACTURERS' AGENTS NATIONAL ASSOCIATION
23016 Mill Creek Road
P.O. Box 3467
Laguna Hills, CA 92654
(714) 859-4040
MARKETING RESEARCH ASSOCIATION
2189 Silas Deane Highway
Suite 5
Rocky Hill, CT 06067
(203) 257-4008
MENSWEAR RETAILERS OF AMERICA
2011 I Street Northwest
Suite 300
Washington, DC 20006
(202) 347-1932
MUSEUM STORE ASSOCIATION
1 Cherry Center
Suite 460
Denver, CO 80222
(303) 329-6968
NATIONAL ADVERTISING AGENCY NETWORK

245 5th Avenue
Suite 2103
New York, NY 10016
(212) 481-3022
NATIONAL-AMERICAN WHOLESALE GROCERS'
ASSOCIATION
201 Park Washington Court
Falls Church, VA 22046
(703) 532-9400
NATIONAL ASSOCIATION FOR PROFESSIONAL
SALESWOMEN
5520 Cherokee Avenue
Suite 200
Alexandria, VA 22312
(703) 256-9226
NATIONAL ASSOCIATION OF BUSINESS AND
INDUSTRIAL SALESWOMEN
90 Corona
Suite 1407
Denver, CO 80218
(303) 777-7257
NATIONAL ASSOCIATION OF BUSINESS
ECONOMISTS
28790 Chagrin Boulevard
Suite 300
Cleveland, OH 44122
(216) 464-7986
NATIONAL ASSOCIATION OF CATALOG SHOWROOM
MERCHANDISERS
P.O. Box 736
East Northport, NY 11731
(516) 754-6041
NATIONAL ASSOCIATION OF CHAIN DRUG STORES
P.O. Box 1417-D49
Alexandria, VA 22313
(703) 549-3011
NATIONAL ASSOCIATION OF COLLEGE STORES
500 East Lorain Street
Oberlin, OH 44074
(216) 775-7777
NATIONAL ASSOCIATION OF CONCESSIONAIRES
35 East Wacker Drive
Suite 1545
Chicago, IL 60601
(312) 236-3858
NATIONAL ASSOCIATION OF CONVENIENCE STORES
1605 King Street
Alexandria, VA 22314
(703) 684-3600
NATIONAL ASSOCIATION OF DISPLAY INDUSTRIES
470 Park Avenue South

17th Floor
New York, NY 10016
(212) 213-2662
NATIONAL ASSOCIATION OF FLOOR COVERING
DISTRIBUTORS
401 North Michigan
Chicago, IL 60611
(312) 644-6610
NATIONAL ASSOCIATION OF FRANCHISE
COMPANIES
221 S.W. 64th Terrace
Pembroke Pines, FL 33023
(305) 966-1530
NATIONAL ASSOCIATION OF MUSIC MERCHANTS
5140 Avenida Encinas
Carlsbad, CA 92008
(619) 438-7327
NATIONAL ASSOCIATION OF PROFESSIONAL
INSURANCE AGENTS
400 North Washington Street
Alexandria, VA 22314
(703) 836-9340
NATIONAL ASSOCIATION OF REALTORS
430 North Michigan Avenue
Chicago, IL 60611
(312) 329-8200
NATIONAL ASSOCIATION OF RETAIL DEALERS OF
AMERICA
10 East 22nd Street
Lombard, IL 60148
(312) 953-8950
NATIONAL ASSOCIATION OF RETAIL DRUGGISTS
205 Daingerfield Road
Alexandria, VA 22314
(703) 683-8200
NATIONAL ASSOCIATION OF WHOLESALER-
DISTRIBUTORS
1725 K Street Northwest
7th Floor
Washington, DC 20006
(202) 872-0885
NATIONAL AUTOMATIC MERCHANDISING
ASSOCIATION
20 North Wacker Drive
Chicago, IL 60606
(312) 346-0370
NATIONAL AUTOMOBILE DEALERS ASSOCIATION
8400 Westpark Drive
McLean, VA 22102
(703) 827-7407
NATIONAL CABLE TELEVISION ASSOCIATION

1724 Massachusetts Avenue Northwest
Washington, DC 20036
(202) 775-3550

NATIONAL COUNCIL OF SALESMEN'S
ORGANIZATIONS
305 5th Avenue
Room 1303
New York, NY 10016
(718) 835-4591

NATIONAL FOOD BROKERS ASSOCIATION
1010 Massachusetts Avenue Northwest
Washington, DC 20001
(202) 789-2844

NATIONAL GROCERS ASSOCIATION
1825 Samuel Morse Drive
Reston, VA 22090
(703) 437-5300

NATIONAL HOME FURNISHINGS ASSOCIATION
P.O. Box 2396
High Point, NC 27261
(919) 883-1650

NATIONAL LUGGAGE DEALERS ASSOCIATION
245 Fifth Avenue
New York, NY 10016
(212) 684-1610

NATIONAL LUMBER AND BUILDING MATERIAL
DEALERS ASSOCIATION
40 Ivy Street Southeast
Washington, DC 20003
(202) 547-2230

NATIONAL MAIL ORDER ASSOCIATION
3875 Wilshire Boulevard
Suite 604
Los Angeles, CA 90010
(213) 380-3686

NATIONAL MOTOR FREIGHT TRAFFIC ASSOCIATION
2200 Mill Road
Alexandria, VA 22314
(703) 838-1810

NATIONAL RETAIL FEDERATION
100 West 31st Street
New York, NY 10001
(212) 244-8780

NATIONAL RETAIL HARDWARE ASSOCIATION
5822 West 74th Street
Indianapolis, IN 46278
(317) 290-0338

NATIONAL SOCIETY OF SALES TRAINING
EXECUTIVES
203 East Third Street
Suite 201

Sanford, FL 32771
(407) 322-3364

NEWSPAPER ADVERTISING BUREAU
1180 Avenue of the Americas
New York, NY 10036
(212) 704-4547

NEWSPAPER ADVERTISING CO-OP NETWORK
10400 Roberts Road
Palos Hills, IL 60465
(708) 662-3010

OUTDOOR ADVERTISING ASSOCIATION OF AMERICA
1212 New York Avenue Northwest
Suite 1210
Washington, DC 20005
(202) 371-5566

POINT-OF-PURCHASE ADVERTISING INSTITUTE
66 North Van Brunt Street
Englewood, NJ 07631
(201) 894-8899

PRIVATE LABEL MANUFACTURERS ASSOCIATION
369 Lexington Avenue
New York, NY 10017
(212) 972-3131

PROMOTION MARKETING ASSOCIATION OF AMERICA
322 Eighth Avenue
Suite 1201
New York, NY 10001
(212) 206-1100

PUBLIC RELATIONS SOCIETY OF AMERICA
33 Irving Place
3rd Floor
New York, NY 10003
(212) 995-2230

RADIO ADVERTISING BUREAU
304 Park Avenue South
New York, NY 10010
(212) 254-4800

RETAIL ADVERTISING CONFERENCE
500 North Michigan Avenue
Suite 600
Chicago, IL 60611
(312) 245-9011

SALES AND MARKETING EXECUTIVES INTERNATIONAL
458 Statler Office Tower
Cleveland, OH 44115
(216) 771-6650

SECURITIES INDUSTRY ASSOCIATION
1255 23rd Street Northwest
Suite 850
Washington, DC 20037
(202) 466-7420

SOCIETY FOR MARKETING PROFESSIONAL
SERVICES
   99 Canal Center Plaza
   Suite 320
   Alexandria, VA 22314
   (703) 549-6117
SOCIETY OF CONSUMER AFFAIRS PROFESSIONALS
IN BUSINESS
   4900 Leesburg Pike
   Suite 400
   Alexandria, VA 22302
   (703) 998-7371
SPECIALTY ADVERTISING ASSOCIATION
INTERNATIONAL
   3125 Skyway Circle North
   Irving, TX 75038
   (214) 252-0404
SUBURBAN NEWSPAPERS OF AMERICA
   401 North Michigan Avenue

Chicago, IL 60611
   (312) 644-6610
TECHNICAL MARKETING SOCIETY OF AMERICA
   4383 Via Majorca
   Cypress, CA 90680
   (714) 821-8672
TELEVISION BUREAU OF ADVERTISING
   477 Madison Avenue
   New York, NY 10022
   (212) 486-1111
TRIAL LAWYERS MARKETING
   1 Boston Place
   Boston, MA 02108
   (617) 742-0696
WOMEN IN ADVERTISING AND MARKETING
   4200 Wisconsin Avenue Northwest
   Suite 106-238
   Washington, DC 20016
   (301) 369-7400